# St.Helens Community Libraries

This book is due for return on or before the last date shown. Fines are charged on overdue books. Renewal may be made by personal application, post or telephone, quoting date, author, title and book number.

| | | |
|---|---|---|
| 29. AUG 13. | | |
| | | |
| 1 9 SEP 2013 | | |
| | | |
| 2 5 NOV 2013 | | |
| 2 0 JUN 2015 | | |
| | | |
| 6 - NOV 2018 | | |
| 8 - OCT 2019 | | |
| | | |
| 1 0 SEP 2021 | | |
| | | |
| | | |

942.7

# WAKES WEEK

## MEMORIES OF
## MILL TOWN HOLIDAYS

When the sands were 'black with people'. Blackpool from the top of the Tower in the summer of 1939, looking down the Golden Mile towards the Central and South Piers.

# WAKES WEEK

## MEMORIES OF
## MILL TOWN HOLIDAYS

John Hudson

ALAN SUTTON

First published in the United Kingdom in 1992 by
Alan Sutton Publishing Limited · Phoenix Mill · Far Thrupp · Stroud·
Gloucestershire

First published in the United States of America in 1993 by
Alan Sutton Publishing Inc · Wolfeboro Falls · NH 03896-0848

British Library Cataloguing in Publication Data

Hudson, John
Wakes Week: Memories of Mill Town Holidays
I. Title
942.7

ISBN 0-7509-0094-6

Library of Congress Cataloging in Publication Data applied for

Typeset in 10/12pt Palatino
Typesetting and origination by
Alan Sutton Publishing Limited
Printed in Great Britain by
The Bath Press, Bath, Avon.

# Contents

# CHAPTER 1

# *A World Turned Upside-Down*

Wakes week: what memories those words stir among people brought up in the Northern textile towns in the years when cotton was king in Lancashire and wool still reigned in the West Riding. Wakes week, when the world was turned upside-down and suddenly all that mattered in life was not how sweetly the loom was running or how well you knew your nine-times table, but the young chap who said he would meet you by the big dipper at eight o'clock or the agony of choosing between a Vimto or a penny cornet at the end of the pier.

What times they were, those years when it seemed that on a date apparently written on tablets of stone the entire town took to the coast and for seven days Blackpool was Oldham-by-Sea and Morecambe became Bradford-super-Mare. Tens of thousands of friends, enemies and relatives were swept seaward by a wave of coaches and trains to rub along together in ways that sometimes made them see each other in an entirely new light, and occasionally changed their lives forever, for better or worse. But of course by no means everybody got away, and those who stayed at home in that strange half-world of a working town at rest did their best to make sure that there was enough going on to convince the peeling-nosed travellers that they had missed all manner of delights when their backs had been turned, from picnics and funfairs to that greatest mystery of all – the way in which the surrounding moorlands, usually grey at best and invisible at worst, suddenly took on hues of green and brown and seemed to hem the town around like big friendly giants as the murk from the factory chimneys died away through the

1

Unchanging human nature: Great Yarmouth sands in the 1890s, as caught by Paul Martin's astonishing candid camera.

week. Today it is increasingly hard to remember when towns like Bolton and Huddersfield, Blackburn and Halifax were islands of smoke and grime, all but cut off from the eyes of the outside world by their aura of filth. But even now, occasionally, long-lost natives return and are start-led by the sight of streets bathed in smoke-free sunshine, the air fit to breathe and the Pennines pin-sharp and clear all around; and when they do, the first words that come to them are almost always the same: 'By heck, it looks like wakes week . . .'

For most people, however, those uniquely communal Northern holi-days mean just one thing: fun. We remember folk long gone, grandmas and aunties, brothers and best pals, and time and time again our happi-est memories of them, memories that colour and enrich our whole way of thinking about them, can be traced back to those annual weeks by the sea. 'Whenever I think of my Uncle Albert I remember one night when

Laughs with the girls from the factory, 1935.

Halifax wakes week visitors to Great Yarmouth, early 1930s.

Blackpool's Golden Mile, 1934: starving newlyweds and on the lamp post, an advertisement for the notorious public humiliation of the Rector of Stiffkey (see Chapter 5).

the pubs were tipping out up by the North Pier at Blackpool,' says Betty
Barker of Preston. 'Uncle was a really fierce teetotaller, a Sunday school
superintendent and churchwarden. He certainly put the fear of God in
me. Anyway, this would have been the early 1930s, when I was about
13, and my elder sister and I had been out with him for an evening stroll
along the more respectable bit of the Prom – no Golden Mile when he
was around – followed by a stop at our usual little café for a cup of
cocoa as a nightcap. We'd fallen a bit behind him, and when we caught
him up he was in the middle of a raging argument with a policeman
and a young chap who was obviously the worse for wear. It was something to do with a cap this man had lost, and for some reason Uncle
Albert had turned into the prize suspect. I don't think the policeman
thought he was for a second, but it seemed that he knew the other chap,
and reckoned that the best way out of it was to be seen to be giving
Uncle a hard time of it.

   '"Now then, old feller, where are you from?" he says.

Boat trip to Blackpool from Barrow-in-Furness, 1912.

'"Preston," says Uncle Albert.

'"Ruddy marvellous," says the policeman. "You can scrape together the fare from Preston, but then you're reduced to pinching the caps from good Blackpool lads' yeds."

'As we walked away I could see Uncle's shoulders shaking, and at first I thought he was in tears. Well, he was, but they were tears of laughter. I'd never seen him remotely like that, and never did again. But for the rest of his days he used to smile about his brush with the law, and speculate on what the parochial church council would have thought about that confrontation at the saloon bar door. I think he was quite proud of it, really. From then on, too, there was never a family gathering when "good Blackpool lads' yeds" didn't creep into the conversation somewhere. I loved and respected old Uncle Albert for all sorts of reasons, but that wakes week night told me all kinds of things about him I'd never have suspected – his deep-down lack of pomposity and his sense of fun.'

Tom Harrington of Leeds tells a sadder story from much the same time, but the message is the same: 'I had a younger brother, Sam. He was a poor little lad, and he died when he was nine. He was loved and cared for by us but he led a miserable life in and out of sanatoriums,

Three shows a day: Cleveleys' Follies of 1938.

When Morecambe still had its Tower, *c.* 1912.

and the only time I remember him really laughing and happy was at Scarborough, playing in the sea and jumping over the waves with a fishing net in his hand. I wish I had a photo of that. I never saw him have so much fun as then.'

'I never saw him have so much fun. . . .' It is a phrase that comes through constantly when Northern folk look back on wakes weeks past, and it is fun that is to the fore in this collection of memories from the golden age of the communal holiday, spanning the years from around the end of the First World War through to the 1950s. Not surprisingly, only childhood memories live on from those earliest years, but from the 1930s onwards we are able to look back on the wakes from all points of view: children, young singles, young couples, families and older holiday-makers. Not everyone plumped for the seaside digs or a stay-at-home holiday, of course, and many mill town folk have warm recollections of weeks in the fresh air – cycling, hiking or getting fell in for a jolly old time of it at those new-fangled holiday camps. We shall also look back at how custom, age-old rights and more enlightened work

More a day for the Golden Mile than the beach: Blackpool, late summer, 1957.

practices combined to set the scene for the wakes week phenomenon in Victorian and Edwardian days, first of all in Lancashire and not long afterwards in the Yorkshire textile towns; but the emphasis remains very much on times within living memory – and on living memories of those times. This is no learned history of the wakes but a mass of impressions of a way of life so recently taken for granted but now lost to us forever.

# CHAPTER 2

# *The World Was So Much Bigger Then*

First there was the looking forward; this was, after all, the one week off of the year, and it meant something more special than almost anything we can imagine today. 'There wasn't much excitement in our lives, but the feeling round the mill in the days leading up to wakes was one of terrific anticipation,' says Ada Fearnley, née Pollard, who started in the spinning department at Standevens in Halifax in the mid-1920s. 'Not that they gave us much time to think about it. The hours were 7 in the morning to 5.15 at night, and if you weren't there before 7.10 a.m. they'd shut the doors for twenty minutes so that you'd lose a full half hour's pay. That was certainly one rule they didn't relax in the week before wakes week, but the last day was a bit different, with cleaning and tidy-ing-up jobs to be done in preparation for the shut-down. Come about 5 o' clock we'd be sidling up towards the door, and if they were feeling generous we might be allowed to begin our holidays five or ten minutes early; but it didn't go beyond that.'

Peggy Hesketh, who left school at 14 in 1925 to work at Chambers' bleach works at Radcliffe, north of Manchester, tells a similar tale: 'Look forward to it? It was all we girls could think and talk about for weeks, especially as five of us used to go off together to Blackpool or Southport or Morecambe. We didn't finish till the Saturday and we just got more and more excited as we went through the ritual of sweeping up and putting sheets over the stocks of cloth for the week. It was special in so many ways, that day, and especially after paid holidays came in. We earned about 30s. a week, and suddenly they'd be putting £3 in your hand, the 30s. you'd earned and another 30s. for doing absolutely nothing apart from going away to the seaside for seven days. We were just over the moon at that. I think some people thought there must be a catch in it, it seemed too good to be true. On top of all that there would be the pay-out at the savings club at the Liberal Club. And for me, on top of that, even, there would be an extra half-crown from the father of a friend of mine, a publican, who'd give me his interest money from the savings club in return for taking his payments in every week. So not only was I going on holiday, but I was feeling flush, too. There was nothing like it, I can tell you.'

Jenny Seddon of Burnley has similar memories, though there was a time when she wondered whether her first wakes away from home would ever happen. 'I started in the weaving sheds when I was 13, but I just gave my mam all my money until I was 16,' she recalls. 'That year I had planned to go away with a friend of mine to Morecambe and we did all the right, sensible things, putting a couple of bob away into going-off clubs and so on. I got the pay-out on the Thursday – and by the time the shops had shut that night I hardly had more than a bob of it left, because I'd needed some new clothes and had just gone mad with this few quid in my pocket, a couple of dresses, a skirt and blouse, shoes, the lot. In the weeks before the holidays the local papers were always packed with advertisements for the dress shops in town, and the prices – 1s. 11d. for a blouse, and so on – looked so tempting when you knew you had that pay-out coming to you. In the end, I think I'd have got about as far as Blackburn on my way to Morecambe, so all I could do was throw myself on the mercy of my mam and dad. There were ructions, of course, but they'd got a bit put aside for something or other they wanted to buy, and they let me have it. Then, after I got back from my whole week away, it was back to handing over most of my pay packet to my mam again for what seemed months on end, until the debt was repaid.'

But the important thing was that Jenny got there, and after the looking forward, that was the next great battle in those days when there were not only no motorways but no cars either, so far as most people were concerned. The world was so much bigger then, and it is not just because we as children were smaller. When you went on a coach trip from the mill towns north of Manchester, your first stop for cups of tea and toilets would be at roadside hotels and barn-like cafés now within perhaps half an hour's drive of home. A favourite stop for travellers from Bolton and Bury to Scarborough was the Triangle pub in West

Blouses from 1s. 11d.: there was always the temptation to spend your going-off club savings before you went away.

**WE STOPPED AT ALL THE PLACES OF INTEREST**

Chara trips did not last long before the first stop.

Yorkshire, on the road between Ripponden and Sowerby Bridge. With the M62, today it takes as long to reach there as it used to do to walk a couple of miles to work or school. A favourite south-bound halt – or a much-used one at least, since a visit there was no treat except for those who like their cuppas best in milling, elbow-jogging throngs – was the huge coach pull-in on the A34 at Newcastle-under-Lyme, near Stoke-on-Trent. The nearest geographical equivalent today is the M6 service station at Keele, well within an hour's run of the South Lancashire towns. Little children and grannies who call for a halt there these days provoke only heavenward glances and stifled sighs among their fellow travellers.

And then there was the sheer joy of those coach rides, for the children at least. While adults might be deep in bickering negotiations about the last half-inch to which a draughty skylight or sliding window might be opened, or later over the volume at which the wireless was acceptable, the kids would be immersed in their own games and songs, at home and at ease among their brothers and sisters and cousins and pals as their little capsule of everyday people sped ever farther from familiar territory. Who would be first to see the sea – or the Tower, if the destination was

Getting away from Longton, near Preston, in the 1920s.

Blackpool? The flat, green Fylde countryside is peppered with pylons, and there cannot be one within sight of the old A583 between Preston and the coast that has not been mistaken for the Tower.

'Seen it, there it is, there it is!'

'Snot. S'just a pylon.'

'Tissen.'

'Tis.'

It is cheering to think that this particular ritual at least has not died, and you can still hear similar learned debates as the coaches bowl out towards Blackpool along the M55. Another custom that lives on is the whip-round for the driver, even though the luxury of his modern working environment, all air-conditioning and radio telephones, makes the collector's job that bit more difficult.

'Tip for t' driver? 'E's earnin' more than me, yon feller.'

'Still, 'e's done a grand job.'

'I'd do a grand job on 'is pay.'

Train journeys, unless your choice of seaside resort was an obvious excursion destination, were always seen as that bit more up-market. The

'Hope our case is still on the roof . . . '. Sunshine greets the latest influx of Blackpool holiday-makers, late 1920s.

Seeing off the chara, 1925.

The race for the train, *c*.1906.

difference in excursion fares might not be more than a few coppers, but if you were off to Blackpool by train and the folks next door were catching the Yelloways, you were the ones more likely to be feeling smug. It is hard, looking back, to imagine why this should be, particularly come the 1950s, when coaches were well sprung and comfortable and the recently nationalized British Railways were still firmly in the era of flying smuts and upholstery that would explode in a storm of dust as you sat down; probably the image owed more to folk memories of the 1920s and '30s and the charas with their hard tyres and spartan seats. It was certainly in the '50s that coach travel took off, with convenient pick-up and drop-off points at either end of the journey proving an added attraction. In Skegness in 1947, for instance, 17 per cent of visitors travelled by car, 16 per cent by coach or bus and 67 per cent by rail. By 1951 a quarter arrived by coach compared with just under 50 per cent by rail, and four years later the three modes of travel were divided almost evenly. If you think that almost one in five visitors sweeping in by car was a suspiciously high figure in 1947, remember that Skegness was one of the great holiday camp resorts, and that you needed a bob or two to stay in those in the early days.

One of the joys of the railway, for children at least, was the way that quite often the trip could turn into a day-long adventure that began at dawn and landed you at your digs hours after the previous week's visitors had been hustled off by the landlady. Sandra Farnworth, who grew up in Rochdale in the 1950s, recalls the extraordinary journey to her aunt's house at Dingle, the tough waterfront suburb of Liverpool where she spent many an improbable but enjoyable wakes week.

'You just wouldn't believe that trip,' she says. 'It seemed to take forever at the time, and looking back, I still can't believe it lasted much less than five hours. That was partly because my dad was always a great one for getting to the station hours before the train was due. More reckless souls could probably have done it in three hours.

'Anyway, there was the ten-minute walk to the bus stop, then the bus down into Rochdale, then the bus from Rochdale into Manchester, and then the hike across town to the railway station. A wait of up to an hour would bring us the train to Liverpool, and after that the fun really started. First of all there was the great once-a-year taxi ride from Lime Street to the Pier Head, which would have been the biggest treat of the holiday had it not been for what was to follow – a ride along to Dingle on that amazing old Victorian overhead railway that gave you a bird's-eye view of the docks. This was in the early 1950s and they were packed with ships, cargo boats with funnels of every colour under the sun and best of all, those stately Cunarders whose red and black funnels we knew so well from pictures of the *Queen Mary* and *Queen Elizabeth*.

'At Dingle there would be the performance all over again, the four of us with our suitcases and haversacks scrambling off the train and setting off on another ten-minute jaunt to my aunt's house. It seemed that the first half hour of our stay was spent just telling her about getting there, which seemed only right; after all, there was plenty to talk about, what with the time it had taken and the variety of transport we'd used.'

Sandra Farnworth still has cousins in that corner of Liverpool. She admits that she is not much in contact with them these days, but when she and her husband Alex drove there along the M62 for a family celebration a few years ago, they completed the trip comfortably within the hour. 'Not that that necessarily made it a better journey,' she insists. 'Shorter, yes, more comfortable, certainly – but will today's children going on holiday by car carry memories of their travels for life, as I remember the old black taxi from Lime Street and those funnels in the docks?'

What Sandra Farnworth and her family tended to miss out on, choos-

The battle of the seaside station in late Victorian times.

ing to spend their holidays in Liverpool, was the vast queues for the trains travelling to more popular holiday hotspots – though in truth the 'Pool could be a busy enough destination in itself when the boats to Douglas and Llandudno were due to sail and New Brighton was in its heyday. Those patient masses of people snaking out of the station booking halls along the cobbled approach road, and more often than not out into the streets themselves; they are another abiding memory of the wakes.

'The holiday started in those queues, though it was a funny way to start a holiday, looking back,' says Janet Carter, a Preston girl whose memories of the classic wakes years stretch from a 1930s childhood to young motherhood in the '50s. 'There were hours to wait, so what with keeping a sharp look-out around you and the kids roaming along the queues and reporting back, you could glean all kinds of information. You'd see such-and-such a family making their way to the station and you'd think: "Golly, I hope they're not coming to Blackpool with us." Or you'd see someone else, someone you knew slightly and felt quite warmly about, and you'd hope they would be on your train, and you might be able to get to know them better over the week.

'For some reason, I always associate those queues at the railway station with drizzle; thick drizzle, the stuff that gets you wet. The smell of wet gabardines and Pacamacs, those plastic concertina Rain Mates up on top of your holiday perm, the rain soaking through your little summer pumps, the relief when you eventually got into the booking hall and out of the weather. Those are the kind of memories I have of queuing for the trains, that and the kids dashing hither and thither bringing us back titbits of news, and all the well-worn buckets and spades lashed to the case handles with string.

'It was only years later, when I moved away from Lancashire, that I realised how odd this was, this great mass exodus we took so much for granted. The idea of a holiday to get away from it all just didn't come into it for most of us. Mill people were a sociable bunch. We worked hard and we played hard and perhaps a bit raucously, though we were disciplined, too, and I never recall much real trouble at Blackpool or Morecambe or the other big resorts we'd go to. I remember a couple who lived just up the road from us just before the war, middle-aged, they seemed to me, though I don't suppose they were much past 30. He had an office job in Blackburn, nothing to do with cotton, and they'd hire a car for their holidays and go off touring in the Lake District or

So this is Blackpool: arriving at Central Station, 1950s.

Scotland. We just couldn't believe this as kids. What kind of a holiday was it if it didn't start early on a Saturday morning in a queue up the station approach and half-way down Fishergate Hill in Preston? I honestly remember us sitting round discussing this weighty topic.'

Ada Fearnley is another with vivid memories of the queues, and the patience with which the long wait for the trains was borne: 'We'd be four or five abreast right up the station approach and up to the top of Horton Street, right into the middle of Halifax, and there'd be no crush or pushing until the very last minute, when you were getting on the train. By 1921 there were eight of us in the family, my parents and six children ranging in age from about 13 down to 3, and that was the first year we all got away together. I remember my father somehow getting us a compartment to ourselves in all the pushing on the platform, and holding the door open as we piled in, four of us on either side. Then off we went to Cleethorpes, never sitting still for long, laughing at each others' black eyes after we'd stuck our heads out of the window and getting our long hair filthy as it streamed out behind us in the smoke.'

The spotting of friends and enemies, the jockeying for seats as near or as far as possible from identified targets, continued in the scramble into the trains. Again, this simple act could set the scene for the week ahead – or in some cases, for considerably longer than that, as Elsie Dowell, a young mother-of-two in Wigan in the 1950s, recalls. 'I had a friend called Annie, walked to the factory every morning and had my dinner with her every day,' she says. 'Unfortunately, my husband knew her chap for some reason, and they didn't see eye-to-eye. As we were making for the train my Dave said:

'"There's that Smith bloke, let's steer well clear of him."

So we moved on a couple of carriages and Annie knew, and I knew, and it was never the same between us again. A similar thing happened to a friend of mine, but in reverse. She and her family got into a compartment with a woman who had fallen out with the girls she was friendly with at the mill. Of course they struck up a conversation, found out they had a lot in common, and spent lots of the following week in Blackpool in each other's company; no need to tell you that that put her in queer street as far as her other workmates were concerned.'

The joys and pains of chance meetings lasted the whole journey through, with whisperings of 'Guess who I've just seen in the buffet' or 'You'll never guess who's just come out of the lav' keeping the wary traveller on his toes to the end; and as the station approached, the surprises didn't finish there. 'I remember a horrific trip to Scarborough on a

'Let's have a cuppa, first': a safe and sunny arrival in 1925.

Mills and Seddon coach from Bury in 1956, when I was 10,' says Michael
Johns. 'When we stopped for refreshments near Halifax I spotted a
vaguely familiar woman and eventually identified her as my headmaster's sister, who'd been in school once or twice helping out. This
reminder of real life didn't please me too much, but it didn't compare
with the gloom that swamped me when I stepped out of the coach at a
gloriously sunny Scarborough and walked into said headmaster waiting
for her. He was in a yellow open-necked shirt and greeted me kindly,
two "firsts" that persuaded me that perhaps people could be nicer on
holiday. But I do remember that the sun didn't shine again that week,
and I couldn't help feeling that old Pop Cook's presence in town had
something to do with it.'

A third form of travel added a romantic dimension to Northern folks'
options if the all-too-often stroppy Irish Sea was not throwing one of its
paddies, for the steamers from Liverpool to the Isle of Man and
Llandudno were the starting point for millions of happy holidays in the
golden years. 'My family holidayed regularly in both Peel on the Isle of
Man and in Colwyn Bay, near Llandudno, in the 1940s and '50s, and the
boat was very much part of it all,' Michael Johns recalls. 'I must say I felt
the Isle of Man boats had much more of a sense of occasion than the old
Liverpool and North Wales Steamship Co. craft, though the seamen on
both lines seemed to wear their embroidered company jerseys with

*St Tudno*, pride of the Liverpool and North Wales Steamship Company's fleet of little ships bound for Llandudno.

pride. The Isle of Man boats looked like proper mini-liners, their red and black funnels an exact replica of the Cunarders' livery, and polished brass and woodwork everywhere. By comparison the *St Tudno*, the pride of the North Wales fleet, always struck me as an ancient craft, low-slung and with a tall, thin smokestack in insipid yellow. As a people-carrier she was a winner, capable of moving seven short of 2,500 shoulder-to-shoulder passengers at a time, but she never stirred me like the *Lady of Mann* and the *Ben-My-Chree* did.' The two golden eras of travel to the island were just before the First World War, when annual return visits comfortably topped the million mark, and the years immediately after the Second. A peak of nine passenger ships operated in the summer of 1955, sailing to Douglas not only the 83 land miles from Liverpool, but from Fleetwood and Heysham, Belfast and Dublin and Ardrossan; the big Scottish engineering towns, after all, had a shutdown holiday tradition comparable in many ways with the Northern wakes, and the Scots-Lancashire mix was one of many strands of life that gave a Manx holiday a flavour of its own.

Michael Johns recalls that an advantage of Llandudno was the relative calm of the crossing: 'I know it's always the done thing to say that

apparently harmless stretches of water can be rough and treacherous –
in Manchester you even hear it said about Heaton Park boating lake –
but I can't really believe that anyone ever had too much trouble cruising
along past the golden and to the eye always sunny sands of Prestatyn,
Rhyl and Colwyn Bay towards Llandudno. We never did, anyway, and
I'd always be up at the prow of the ship as the pier drew nearer and
nearer. The Isle of Man could be a very different kettle of fish, and I
remember some evil trips over there, both as a child in the '40s and as a
young man later on, times when I would gladly have swapped a swift
and painless death for what I was going through. My mother was no
great sailor; she still talks of an outward voyage aboard the old *Manx
Maid* in the late 1940s, and the hours she spent praying on holiday that it
would be a different boat when we came home. She swears the *Manx
Maid* stood on its nose in the trough of a wave at one point, water towering up all around her. My blackest memories are of a midnight special
over to Douglas during Bury wakes in the early '60s. I was with a gang
of lads and we'd done plenty of drinking before we staggered up the
gangway, as had almost everybody else aboard. We were no sooner out
in Liverpool Bay, where there were nearly as many wrecks in the sea as
there were on the boat, than we realized it was going to be a rough
crossing. There were some horrible sights aboard that night, and though
I'm no great art critic, when we eventually landed up in a saloon in the
bowels of the boat I was reminded irresistibly of paintings by Hier-
onymus Bosch, the old Dutchman who used to specialize in pictures of
poor tormented creatures writhing in hell.'

Michael Johns' mother was right to be chary about sailing back to
Liverpool on the first *Manx Maid*. By the late '40s she was very much the
veteran of the fleet, a survivor of two World Wars dating from 1910 –
when she had been a railway company boat called the *Caesarea*. She
transferred to the Isle of Man colours in 1923 but was always tiny by
their standards, carrying 1,600 passengers compared with the 1930-built
*Lady of Mann*'s 3,000. Immediately after the war and for the next ten
years Cammell Laird started building the company a new class of ship,
neat and compact craft like the *King Orry*, *Tynwald*, *Snaefell* and *Manx-
man*, but the call for island holidays was such that the classic mini-liners,
the *Lady of Mann* and the 1927 veteran the *Ben-My-Chree*, were as busy as
ever – and on the real high days and holidays, out puffed the dreaded
*Manx Maid*. Her end came shortly after the Johns family's unhappy
experience with her, in 1950, when she was sold for scrap – an event also
recalled by Michael Johns.

'My father must have seen a paragraph in a newspaper somewhere to the effect that she had been scrapped,' he says. 'Of course she was still fresh in our minds in those days, and he would always be telling us children that she had been chopped up into razor blades. If he had had a particularly bad shave one morning he would dab the nicks with a piece of toilet paper and say: "By gum, that was a rough 'un. Must have been a bit of the old *Manx Maid.*"'

Happily, Michael Johns' most abiding memories of the Isle of Man crossing stem from his early childhood, and the sheer magic of sailing off on holiday on a real ship from one of the great seaports of the world. 'There were always things to terrify a four-year-old, like a ship's hooter blaring out and those great tobacco pipe-shaped ventilators with their gaping red mouths,' he recalls. 'But these were risks well worth running compared with exploring the ship and striding around the decks pretending to be captain and hoping that one, just one, passenger might take you to be him. Later, when I was aged from about 8 to 14, the occasion would give my dad his annual opportunity to trot out his two Liverpool docks jokes. One, inspired by the ships' names *Mona's Isle* and *Mona's Queen*, was:

'"Who painted the Mona Lisa?"

'"Cammell Laird. They do all the Isle of Man boats."

'And the other was:

'"Where's the urinal?"

'"I don't know, but I think it's that one over there with the two blue funnels."

'In the mid-1980s I had to visit a firm on Birkenhead docks on business, and was amazed to see two of the vintage Isle of Man steamers laid up there. It was a wide, bleak stretch of water, empty but for these craft, and when I walked the couple of hundred yards over to take a closer look at them it was a depressing sight. They looked tired and shabby, and they seemed to have attracted all the oil and debris in the dock to lap up around them. I was walking back to my business colleagues in a sad state of mind until I saw a man coming up towards me and suddenly started hoping that he'd ask me the way to the urinal. Of course we passed each other without a word, but the thought of that old joke cheered me, and took me back to the days when those two old tubs almost land-locked behind me in the dock would happily take on the worst the Irish Sea could throw at them.'

In the post-war years the *St Tudno* had two smaller but still venerable sister ships, the *St Seriol* and the *St Trillo*, the *Seriol* being distinguished

Mini-liners: the Isle of Man Steam Packet Company's *Lady of Mann* and *Ben-My-Chree*.

by the fact that she was the only one the English passengers could pronounce with any semblance of accuracy; older travellers recall the *Marguerite*, but by the 1960s the three Saints passed into history alongside her, and sailings were taken over briefly by the Isle of Man boats until they, too, found the service no longer viable. Now the only pleasure ships that put in to Llandudno's lofty pier are the *Waverley* and the *Balmoral*, those two veterans that dot around the shores of Britain during the summer months, bringing us a fleeting reminder of the sailing days.

For travellers by ferry in the inter-war years to New Brighton, then a big, brash, tough resort that played Coney Island to Liverpool's New York, there was the bonus of the bizarre welcome awaiting them courtesy of Peggy, the one-legged diver. Peggy of course was a man, his nickname being a laconic Scouse tribute to the peg leg he wore when not going about his trade. But what a man, and what a trade. He would wait until the boat was approaching the jetty and then, seconds away from that familiar moment when wooden pier, steel ship side, and old rubber tyres and plaited rope fenders came together with crunches and creaks and groans, he would plunge gracefully into the murky depths between them. Women screamed. Children laughed, as children will when seeing grown men do daft things that imperil their lives. Other grown men shuddered. But seconds later the gangplank would be down, the crowds would be surging off the ship to taste the delights of the Tower and the funfair and all else that New Brighton had to offer. And there at the end, determined but moist, in the splendid words of that Marriott Edgar monologue about the man who swam from Bury to Blackpool Tower to escape Noah's flood, was a dripping Peggy, cap in hand. Many people will remember his greeting, even if they never met the man. 'Don't forget the diver, sir, don't forget the diver,' he would intone, and before long it was a little bit of folklore among trippers to the resort.

Someone who knew it well was the Liverpudlian comedian Tommy Handley, star of the war-time and late 1940s radio show *ITMA* – and in a half-hour that often seemed to consist of no more than catchphrases strung one after another, there was nothing more calculated to send the audience into paroxysms of mirth than 'Don't forget the diver'. In the show the diver was played by Horace Percival, who also had them rolling in the aisles with such shafts of wit as 'Every penny makes the water warmer' and 'I'm going down now, sir'. But not for us to reason why one generation should fall about at commonplaces that leave the next stone cold. Suffice it to say that Peggy also reaped rewards from all this unexpected fame, for in those heady years after the war ended he was called upon to practise his craft not in the oily depths of Liverpool Bay but off the graceful art deco diving boards of the major holiday camps. He even put out postcards, happily describing himself as 'the one-legged diver', and the campers queued three deep to have him sign them with a flourish. Best of all, his wish really did come true; because of Tommy Handley and his legacy, the diver will not be forgotten.

# CHAPTER 3

# *Use Of Cruet Extra*

What would the digs be like? Of course a lot of us knew, since they'd be just as they were the previous year and the year before that. The room would be the same, the landlady would be the same and the other families down the corridor would be the same. That was the essence of wakes week for so many, a break with routine but with familiarity and reassurance all around. If you did decide to change resort – 'Let's give Cleethorpes a bash next time' – it would be with a view to granting it an extended run, if you liked it, for another clutch of years of your life. To lots of families, not to go back was seen as a tacit admission that you had not enjoyed your last holiday – which would be a bit rich after you had gone home telling the neighbours how marvellous it had been. You also ran the risk of appearing stand-offish, breaking away from the group of friends, neighbours and other fellow townsfolk with whom you had spent and apparently enjoyed your last holiday. Most of all, it paid to stick with a landlady you knew and could get on with, when you heard all the horror stories from other families you bumped into on the beach or along the Prom. All those comic postcards about hunting bedbugs and being greeted on the doorstep by stony-faced old harridans in curlers – there was a grain of truth in them. Those cards would not have sold in their millions if that had not been case. Neither would Keatings powder, with which to wage war on bugs, have been such a consistent advertiser in seaside newspapers. In the circumstances, 'spotlessly clean' tended to be the highest compliment you could pay your digs or your landlady, along with her ability to tot the bill up correctly at the end of the week. Any social graces over and above these two were much to be prized – but basic cleanliness and honesty more often than not won her the reward of your going back year after year, usually by booking your return visit before your current one had ended.

The battle of the bedbugs, 1908.

If you did opt for pastures new, booking could not have been easier. Word-of-mouth recommendation was the best way of tracking down fresh digs, but if all else failed, guest houses and apartments would be advertised by the yard every day in the small ads columns of big Northern 'national' newspapers like the Manchester-based *Daily Dispatch*. 'The usual thing was to pay so much for the use of a bed for the night,' says Joan Bowles, née Birkby, who was brought up in the Chesham area of Bury between the wars. 'When we stayed at West Kirby and later at Llanfairfechan, the rate was around 4s. a night. You'd do your own shopping, with your own cupboard in the dining room, and you'd either eat out or the landlady would cook your food for you. The first time we went full board was in Bury wakes in August 1939, before they switched the week to July. We went to Bridlington and really thought we were going quite up-market spending 8s. 6d. a day. We felt it was the kind of lifestyle we could get used to, but, of course, we weren't given the chance for a few years. All through the holiday we could hear gunfire out at sea as the Navy went through their manoeuvres, and my dad would say: "There's going to be a war." No sooner had we got home than the announcement was made by Mr Churchill,

The landlady as ogress, *c.* 1930.

and if it was possible for anyone to get any pleasure out of something like that, I think my dad did when he thought back to the gunfire off Bridlington and said: "What did I tell you?"'

Dads were wont to make ominous pronouncements on holidays, still remembered decades later. Ada Fearnley of Halifax recalls the last time she and her parents, four sisters and brother were photographed all together, in Cleethorpes in the mid-1920s: 'My father was very uneasy about it, he didn't like the idea at all. He wasn't a superstitious man but he said: "When you do this kind of thing there's always one missing the next time." I don't know whether he had anyone in particular in mind, but sadly he was right. By the time the next holiday came around my sister Nellie, the third of the six of us, had died at 14.'

Enterprising grocery chains with branches far and wide cashed in on that odd arrangement by which landladies cooked the guests' own food by inviting customers to put their usual order in at their local shop – and hey, presto! – the provisions would be delivered to their digs via the shop's seaside branch. The James Duckworth chain, for example, one of those grand old firms in the Maypole, Seymour Mead and Burgons mould, where the air was always heavy with the smell of smoked bacon, Cheddar cheese and huge pats of fresh butter, made the most of its four branches in the Blackpool and St Anne's area to make life easier for holiday-makers. The exercise did not take too much organizing, after all, involving nothing more than a phone call from the inland branch to the coastal shop; but in the 1920s it seemed a very smart piece of business, and one that could only be good for customer relations. Looking back to the 1950s, Michael Johns also recalls the pitfalls of the bring-your-own food system. 'My parents were not great ones for involving us children in the nuts and bolts of running the family,' he recalls. 'They took the very sensible view that as long as we were fed and happy, it didn't matter to us how the meal got on the table. The first time I realized that this was the way our holiday catering worked was when we were staying in Cleveleys in about 1957, and towards the end of the week the landlady asked me to tell my mum and dad that we needed another quarter of tea. I didn't think a lot about it, but when I passed the message on, it was rather as if I had told them that the rent had gone up to £1,000 a week, or Colorado beetles had been found on my dad's allotment. They hit the roof, and there was this huge inquest with the landlady over how a quarter of tea that usually lasted us however many weeks could have gone in a few days. The rest of the week passed with exchanges of icy politeness whenever we saw her and, needless to say, that was one lot of

Home-from-home service, Rochdale wakes, 1923.

digs we didn't go back to again. Not that the landlady was forgotten, not least because of the coincidence that my dad's favourite expression for "thief" was the Cockney rhyming slang "tea leaf". The poor woman went down in family history as a purloiner of innocent travellers' tea, but at least she hadn't put us down for a few coppers at the end of the week for "use of cruet", a hidden extra that often sent my parents into even greater paroxysms of fury.

'Looking back, those landladies who cooked the guests' own food were on a hiding to nothing. Producing the exact meals the visitors had at home, they were expected to make it taste just the way mum made it, and no two people cook the same. I suppose that added to the image of the landlady being a rotten cook, kids going around wrinkling up their faces and saying "Urrrgh, that dinner was vile" if the potatoes or carrots were boiled a couple of minutes longer than what they were used to, or if she'd got Daddies sauce instead of HP when she had bought the order we'd sent her to be waiting for us when we arrived. They were another minefield, those orders. I remember one landlady buying smoked bacon instead of plain, enough to last us three or four breakfasts, and every morning there'd be the same old muttered protests. And if she'd paid $9\frac{1}{2}$d. for biscuits we could have got for 9d. at home . . .'

How landladies would cater for today's faddy generation in such circumstances is difficult to imagine, but picture a breakfast order along the lines of: 'I'm into plain yoghurt and honey, but my husband Chris likes a full English breakfast, grilled not fried, and Darren's a porridge and banana boy and Tracey's on a no-wheat diet with skimmed milk and plenty of fibre. It's decaffeinated coffee for me, but Chris can only take a strong filter and Darren. . . .'

The other side of the coin was that if you did hit upon a landlady and her family you got on with, going back annually could be like staying with friends, apart from the settling-up ritual at the end of the week. 'We went back to the same place year after year, up behind the Imperial Hotel in Blackpool,' says Alan Smith of Whitefield, near Manchester. 'It was a family called Thompson, and in the end we got to going on little outings with them, just as if they were fellow holiday-makers. One year, when I was six or seven, Mrs Thompson found a fishing reel some previous guest had left behind, one of those square frames you wrapped the line around. I must have been going on about wanting to go fishing, because as soon as they found this thing there was a great song and dance about our all going out to try it out, and the excitement built up over the next couple of days as the landlady made a batch of sugar bait.

In the end, out we all trooped to the Promenade at high tide; my father carefully unravelled a long length of line, swung it over his head, let go with expert timing – and watched in horror with the rest of us as the whole lot came loose from the frame he was holding and disappeared in the deep. The line had apparently been attached to the wooden reel by string that had rotted over the years; but at that age I was in no mood for rational discussion about the whys and wherefores, and my parents recalled for years the look of bemused indignation on my face as the tackle vanished over the sea wall.'

Ada Fearnley of Halifax remembers another phenomenon of the time, the single-sex boarding house: 'When we were young adults my brother and sisters and I would still go on holiday together, with partners coming along too, as we became engaged and married. In the early '30s my future husband Les joined us for the first time in Great Yarmouth, and there was no room for him in the little apartment house we took over. He stayed instead at a men-only hotel called the Garibaldi – it's a name I'll never forget, because all the residents wore little sailor caps with "Garibaldi" on them.'

It was a case of all girls together when Peggy Hesketh and four of her bleach mill workmates from Radcliffe, north of Manchester, shared an attic in Blackpool in the late 1930s. 'We were not too impressed when the landlady first showed us up to it,' she says. 'But it was even worse the first night it rained, and the water came pouring through. We had a laugh about it later, but it was really no joke at the time. Though we didn't have much money to pay, we deserved better than that.'

But a happy memory of seaside digs to end the chapter, in the form of a poem called *Wakes Week* by one of our leading current Lancashire dialect writers, Joan Townsend, née Pomfret, of Great Harwood. Joan Pomfret has an ear for a poignant phrase as keen as any poet's in the land – and nothing could ring more true than that glorious: 'We's be i' Peel toneet!'

> Summer meant packin' th'owd tin trunk
> An' tekkin' t'cat next dooar;
> T'gas torned oaf, th'aspidistra degged,
> Buckets an' spades on t'flooar.
> Mi Mother i' her Sunda' best
> Shivin' up egg an' beet
> Fer t'sandwiches – an' t'last mad rush
> As t'cab crawled up eawr street!

Summer meant fidgetin' i' train
As t'teawn wor left behind,
An' gerrin' slapped fer muckyin' up
Mi honds on t'strap o' t'blind.
We allus knew when t'say wor near,
T'sky seeomed so blue an' breet;
An' once on t'ship me dad ud say:
'We's be i' Peel toneet!'

Ah corned think why we went so far,
A weyk were noan so lung –
But eh, Ah'm glad we did! Id wor
A grand place to be young!
Fer ther' wor fishin' booats on t'tide
An pratty shells on t'shore,
An' gret gulls skrikin' – aye, an' fleawrs
Ah'd niver sin afore!

We allus lodged at Missus Moore's,
'Sea View', on th'edge o' t'bay;
Went charra thrips to Douglas Head
An' Ramsey an' Glen Maye.
Summer meant smellin' kipper smooak,
Sand-pies an' songs an' fun –
Mi Mother, set on t'Castle rocks,
Her bonny face to t'sun.

T'weather worned like id is today,
'Twor allus lovely then,
An' t'magic stayed till th'owd tin trunk
Wor fastened up agen.
Id's o' past histhory neaw – an' yet
When Memory's lamp's aleet,
Ah fancy Ah still yer Dad say:
'We's be i' Peel toneet!'

# CHAPTER 4

# *We've Come All This Way . . .*

The most celebrated chance meeting of near neighbours on holiday came in *Hindle Wakes*, a play by Stanley Houghton first staged in 1912. It told of a poor Lancashire mill lass's encounter with her boss's son on a bank holiday excursion to Blackpool, her weekend with him in Llandudno soon afterwards, and all that ensued from those hapless events; a cautionary tale still much beloved of Northern rep and amateur dramatic companies, and not one with many laughs. In real life, though, Harry Bradshaw of south-east Lancashire found the meeting of neighbours on the Prom or down on the sands far more entertaining than Houghton's sad scenario. 'The first time you saw someone you weren't absolutely sure would be at the same resort as you, there would be a tremendous fuss made,' he recalls. '"Well, I never did"; "Fancy seeing you"; "By gum, it's a small world." Honestly, it was like Livingstone meeting Stanley, even though, deep down, you knew the other folks must be on holiday the same time as you, and that it wasn't the most staggering thing in the world for them to have chosen Morecambe, or Blackpool, or wherever you happened to be. It was just one of those funny little rituals I remember.' A variation of the theme would be: 'We've come all this way to get away from you'; and if, as often happened, families on a week's holiday arranged to meet up midweek with stay-at-home friends on a day trip, the first question would never vary from: 'What's the weather like at home? It's been gorgeous here.' This last phrase was a statutory part of the formula, even if the footpaths were still moist and mum was carrying a beach bag full of damp and steaming Pacamacs.

I HAVE FOUND A ~~GIRL~~ *boy*
WHO LOVES ME

FOR 10 DAYS ONLY

Celia posted the card to Maggie in 1912, but did not elaborate on the message.

Graham Evans of Huddersfield remembers a rather more original greeting on the front at Skegness just before the last war: 'We were walking along by the sea when my dad spotted a workmate of his at the mill, a chap called Tom Christie, sitting alone reading a paper in a deckchair but surrounded by dozens of other people. Now old Tom was a bit of a joker and very quick on the uptake, so my dad walked up to him and said in a loud voice:

'"You are Lobby Lud and I claim my £5 prize." With scarcely a second's hesitation Tom looked up and said equally loudly:

'"You've got me there, sir, it's a fair cop," and there was much fumbling around with his wallet making as if to give my dad the money. Of course by this time everyone around was sitting up and taking notice, and those who had got a copy of the paper Lobby Lud was working for at that time was kicking themselves for not having challenged him. What amazed me was the straight faces both my dad and Tom Christie

Unisex costumes but most definitely mixed bathing in Edwardian times.

kept right through all this rigmarole, though I believe they used to have a laugh at it at work for years after.'

The real Lobby Lud was indeed one of those people who could leave you kicking yourself in the golden years of the wakes – the mystery man in your resort that very day who would part with a fiver or even more if you waved a copy of his employers' newspaper under his nose and were word-perfect with the magic words. But word-perfect, there was the rub. To pick the right man out of the tens of thousands on the beach and then make a pig's ear of the challenge and miss out on perhaps £50 – twenty weeks' pay to most people pre-war – was calculated to ruin not only your holiday but the rest of the year. Mr Lud was the brainchild of some bright circulation man at the *Westminster Gazette* in August 1927, the name coming from the paper's telegraphic address – Lobby for politics and thus Westminster and Lud from Ludgate Circus. As a matter of fact the circulation man was perhaps not so bright, since the *Gazette* folded in the following year, and its prizes of £50 going up weekly every time they were unclaimed were proved ridiculously high by the newspapers that took up the stunt. The *Daily News* and later the *News Chronicle* generated just as much interest and publicity by offering mere fivers and tenners. The resorts generally were happy hunting grounds

East Coast stalwarts: the *Yorkshireman* at Bridlington, *c.*1934 and the *Southend Belle* up country from her old haunts at Great Yarmouth, 1927.

Halifax girls in the swim, *c.*1930.

for the national press, whose circulation war between the 1930s and '50s was every bit as fierce as today's, but it is intriguing that Mr Lud, the most high-profile undercover man of all time, saw all three of his papers die on him. It was a different tale for Flook, the other great Fleet Street character to be seen on the seashores of Britain at that time. He and his beach sports for the kiddies helped the *Daily Mail* win many a circulation battle over the years – but the little elephant's eventual reward from his bosses was a firm directive to pack his trunk and leave the paper's pages to more trendy beings.

Joan McKichan, brought up in south Lancashire but now living in Aberdeen, remembers a time when someone from home was by no means keen to see her: 'After I left school, my first job was in the drawing office of the local town hall. On holiday that first summer I bumped into one of the waitresses from the staff canteen, and I could tell instantly that she wasn't exactly overjoyed to see me. She was with some people I didn't know, and with her bravest smile she introduced me to them saying:

North Wales favourites: Penmaenmawr and Abergele.

'"This is a lady who comes into the gown shop where I work."

'Well, it surprised me. To my mind she didn't have a bad job. She was quite a senior waitress working in pleasant conditions, no kitchen skivvy, and to this day I can't see why she felt she had to lie about her job – and if she did, why she had decided to be an assistant in a dress shop rather than a brain surgeon or at least the personal secretary to one of the big mill owners.'

Then there was the kicking-yourself-for-the-rest-of-the-week school of chance meetings, of the kind still remembered ruefully by Pat Lowe of Wigan: 'We were on holiday in Llandudno just before the war, staying in a little terrace up behind the Empire Hotel, on the side of the Great Orme. There was a couple who lived next door to us at home, the Wilsons, and they'd been feeling a bit down in the mouth because for some reason or other they'd not got a summer holiday sorted out and were just going off on days. As a matter of fact, they were always down in the mouth about something, and my parents didn't enjoy their company very much at all. Anyway, on about the third day of our holiday, my mother sent them a postcard saying wish you were here, and all that, and my dad, like a fool, put a pin-prick through the panoramic view of Llandudno showing where our digs were, right up on the hillside. They posted the card at about four in the afternoon on the Monday. Just after dinner on the Tuesday we were all trooping down the steep steps from our digs into town when we were confronted by these two chillingly familiar figures loaded up with suitcases and carrier bags and what have you. They must have studied that damned postcard with a microscope to track us down to the street, but track us down they had done.

'"It were such a nice card, and I says to Jim, well, why not?" says Ma Wilson.

'So of course we were lumbered with them for the rest of the week from then on. Truth to tell, they were better company than my parents expected, and they all got on better together for the rest of their lives after that. In fact, after my dad died, the Wilsons were really good to my mother, taking her out on outings and helping her with the shopping, and it was all down to that wakes week; but it was still a rotten shock seeing them at the time.'

Peter Walmsley of Rochdale remembers a more pre-planned meeting with neighbours on a day trip from home. 'The main wakes holidays in Rochdale have swapped about so much over the years, and there was a time in about 1930 when they moved from August to late July, with a

All dressed up and somewhere to go. Halifax holidaymakers out on the town at Great Yarmouth and Skegness.

September break,' he says. 'This infuriated my dad because he was a fanatic for his allotment. That third week of July was just about the peak time for his veg, and he feared he would be putting in months of effort just to see the stuff rot in the ground or be snapped up by neighbours. The upshot was, when we went away to Southport that first year of the July week we went not just with suitcases but with a potato sack full of greens to put with our other provisions in the landlady's cupboard – and then, midweek, when our next-door neighbours came to see us on a day trip, they brought another great bagful to see us through the rest of the week. I read in a newspaper a few years ago about a family from up here somewhere going away on holiday with a trunk full of shelled peas. The newspaper thought it was funny, but I think my dad would have seen the sense in it.'

There was humiliation upon humiliation when Margaret Dean of Leeds and her friend Elsie tried to cheat the turnstile at a ladies lavatory in Whitby in 1956. 'I always resented those turnstiles, always felt women were shabbily treated compared with the men, long before any-one had ever heard of Women's Lib,' she says. 'Usually, when they were waist-high, the agile could climb over them, but this one was floor to ceiling with a metal cage around it. Determined to salvage some saving

Not too choppy - so far. Boat trippers in the late 1920s.

out of it, Elsie and I squeezed together into one section and put in our single penny. It moved a little bit, and then it stuck tight. We couldn't move it in either direction, and let alone getting in, we couldn't even beat a retreat and get out. The toilets were right on the corner of a street, and by this time people had twigged what was going on, and how we had been well and truly caught out. What made it worse was when a gang of girls from our mill, who were staying just up the road from us, came along and discovered this unseemly scene. Well, you can imagine, they just died laughing, and it was not long before that's what we were doing, too. In the end we were so weak with laughter that we couldn't have pushed the turnstile with any force to save our lives – but fortunately we discovered that it was my raincoat belt that was gumming up the works. After I had pulled it out of the mechanism we gave one of the girls another penny to put in and moved majestically into the lavs – at the going rate of a penny each.'

Albert Deeley of Blackburn knew that his local vicar was going off for the wakes along with most of the rest of his flock in that vintage post-war summer of 1947 – but he was still shocked to see the gentleman of the cloth walking towards him along the front at Morecambe, not only in a mauve shirt but minus his dog-collar, no less. 'I could never take the man seriously after that,' says Albert. 'I can't begin to describe what a let-down it was, almost like discovering there was no Father Christmas.' Like many of his generation, Albert attended Sunday school while he was on holiday, making sure his record book was signed at the end of it to ensure that he kept in the race for the good attendance prize at the end of the year, and qualified for the full set of beautiful coloured stamps his home Sunday school gave away week by week. 'I didn't mind doing it, never felt I was missing out on my holiday, because I found it fun to meet up with all the different children,' he recalls. 'Nevertheless, there was one year, in Peel on the Isle of Man in the late '40s, when I felt I earned my attendance credits pretty easily. The first Sunday we'd no sooner started when the lifeboat maroon went up and all the kids tore out to watch the launching. I suppose half of them had dads or uncles aboard, so you could hardly blame them. That was Sunday school over for that week, anyway, and the next week there wasn't one at all – but I was told that if I really wanted my card signed, I should go round to the clergyman's house for his signature. That I did, which meant that after a total of about five minutes of Sunday school I'd qualified for two weeks' attendances, which I didn't think was bad going. What I do remember about the vicar's house was a glass case in

'I thought we'd left Great Aunt Maud round here somewhere. . . .' Blackpool beach, 1958.

Looking spruce on Blackpool Prom, 1930s.

'We prefer a bit of peace. . . '. Halifax
trippers, 1930s.

Round the bay and back for tea: Cleethorpes, 1921.

the hall full of butterflies stuck down with pins. I thought how could he, a man of God, stick pins in His beautiful creatures like that? That was something only nasty little lads like me were supposed to do. What with our vicar's mauve shirt a couple of years earlier, and now this one's butterflies, I didn't know whether I was coming or going.'

But it was far away from the Sunday school – in the dark, steaming dance halls with their mirror globes flecking the couples with stardust, or at large on the fairylit Prom at night – where the girls and boys from the mill towns always dreamed of making their most memorable chance encounters of the holiday. Quite what they got up to has been the subject of many a learned sociological thesis – as well as the notorious Mass-Observation survey of Blackpool in 1937 and '38 when teams of young researchers, many of them middle-class Oxford students, descended on a resort that had never underplayed its hand at hinting at the sexual possibilities of life on its packed beaches and in those dimly lit bars and ballrooms. Their account of their efforts to learn the truth makes wonderfully entertaining reading, and it seems today an odd kind of survey, one in which its participants were fully aware of the slightly absurd nature of their task – and of the possibility, in their role as *agents provocateurs*, of themselves becoming part of the Shocking

Manchester girls on Morecambe Pier,
1961.

Statistics. 'Observer units combed the sands at all hours,' they recorded. '. . . Crawled around under the piers and hulkings, pretended to be
drunk and fell in heaps on located sand couples to  feel what they
were doing exactly, while others hung over the sea wall and railings
for hours watching couples in their hollowed-out sandpits below.
Lines of observers systematically beat the notorious sand dunes . . .'

And what did they find? Well, on one night between 11.30 p.m. and
midnight they discovered 232 couples up to something, but not one of
them going beyond kissing and embracing. At the end of several weeks
of this earnest research, in fact, they had recorded just four cases of full
sex – one of them involving one of their own number, obviously intent
on doing his or her bit to salvage something of Blackpool's raffish reputation. The popular press interpreted such findings as proof that the
playground of the North was in fact 'the most moral town in England',

Mighty mean hombres: Lancashire lads at the Wild West bar, Douglas Bay Hotel, early 1960s.

perhaps not quite what those whose task it was to promote the place really wanted to hear, deep in their hearts. And the observers set great store by a conversation they had with an all-night coffee-stall holder on the Prom after they had staggered up from another weary night combing the dunes. Down there on the sands right now, he told them, there were thousands, and most of them would be there right through the night: 'In fact, there were three couples.'

There are latter-day Jack-the-lads who grew up in Blackpool who will dispute these findings, and say that when the annual list of wakes weeks was published they would be down at the pub on Saturday night saying 'Rochdale's here this week, they went some last year,' and so on. One youth, it was said, even went so far as to rent a garage not far from the Prom at half a crown a week, and created his own little seduction parlour by installing a settee in it. The Winter Gardens, the Tower Ballroom, the piers, they were the places to pick them up, they recall, independent-minded mill girls in gangs of five or six, hell-bent on enjoying themselves and with a bit of brass in their pockets. And as for the Mass-Observation toffs and their findings, well, they just did not understand sex and how quickly and furtively it happened on Blackpool

Such happy smiles in the briny.

sands and up the little backstreet alleyways. Mad, passionate love it wasn't. The true picture doubtless lies between these contrasting accounts – though one reminder that we are talking about a world very different from our own lies in the fact that in all of 1936 there were just seventy-six babies born out of wedlock in Blackpool – and that average of just over six per month gave the town the highest illegitimate birth rate in England. The memories of Peggy Hesketh, who loved nights out at the Tower and the Winter Gardens with the four Radcliffe bleach works girl friends she went away with, certainly tally more with the Mass-Observation than with the Jack-the-lad school. 'Oh, there was a lot of talk,' she says. 'There were always girls who liked to boast that such-a-lad did this or said that, but we never believed them, and they knew we never believed them. It was like a game. They'd have been horrified to think that we ever could have believed them.'

# CHAPTER 5

# *It's Turned Out Nice Again*

They say there's no business like show business, and you could easily feel there was no business other than show business at the big resorts during wakes week in the golden years. Theatres, concert parties, fun-fairs, gaming machines, gypsy fortune tellers, Dutch auctions, street photographers, shellfish stalls, cafés, bars, restaurants. . . . They even made an entertainment out of weighing you and telling you you were too fat – or more often, in the 1920s, too skinny, hard though it may be to believe now: 'Eat up yer crusts and yer greens like yer mam says, young feller. They'll put hairs on yer chest, yer know.' Part of the deal was that the scales attendant would guess your weight first, feeling your shoulders and generally eyeing you up from top to toe, and if he was more than a few pounds out either way he would give you a small prize, or at least your money back. 'I always used to beat them when I was in my teens,' Joan McKichan, a south-east Lancashire girl, recalls. 'I looked skinny, but deep down I must have been quite well built. Well, if you must know, I now know that I'm quite well built. Whatever, the men on the scales would always weigh me up and underestimate me by a stone or more, so I'd get their free gift, usually a little metal brooch; in Blackpool it was a pin with the Tower on it. Needless to say, the prize you won if you beat the system was worth far less than the money you'd paid out in the first place. That's my abiding memory of the sea-side showmen. They won even when they lost.'

Farther up the entertainment scale, the major resorts would vie with each other for the summer show 'names' who would put the bums on

Blackpool Pleasure Beach in the 1930s. The ferris wheel was not big but neither was the fare, at 2d. a go.

A sensation in around 1904: the 40 m.p.h. Maxim Flying Machine, seen at Southport and Blackpool.

seats in pier-end and promenade theatres night after night. Three-month bookings at a single hall by the sea were a blessing for the acts that slogged around the northern Variety circuit houses a week at a time for the rest of the year, and admirers who followed their fortunes would swear that the big-name singers and comedians were never on better form than a couple of weeks into a successful seaside season. More often than not the top artists would rent a pleasant house in the resort, install their family and friends there and regard the entire summer as a well paid holiday with the not inconsiderable bonus of a massage for the ego twice nightly by thousands of adoring fans. In the words of a song well known in their circle, it was *Nice Work If You Can Get It*.

In the days of Variety it was the comedians who were in greatest demand. George Formby loved Blackpool as much as Blackpool loved George, who had first appeared at the Palace in 1921 and was almost a fixture during the '30s; the coach operators even included his posh house down at St Anne's on their tour of notable sights, a sure sign that an artist had hit the big time. It is odd to think that the man who made a fortune by singing about being a window cleaner peeping in through other people's panes should be the subject of similar scrutiny on a mass scale, as chara after chara slowed down to let its passengers strain to catch a glimpse of what we now know was not always serene life behind the neat net curtains of Beryldene. There was always a place by the sea, too, for Frank Randle, the thin-faced, rough Wigan lad with just about every vice in the book to set alongside his saving grace of being able to make people laugh. As was the way with most artists in those days of set Variety circuits, he rarely strayed south to the London halls; those with scant regard for his talents would say it was only fair that Frank Randle should be restricted to the North as the South had had to put up with the doodlebugs, but his paying customers never stopped falling off their seats at his summer shows at the Palace, where he topped the bill from 1934 to '39. Alan Smith of Whitefield best remembers the Variety bill on the North Pier at Blackpool, *On With The Show*, though the amazing Randle also stands out in his memory: 'He wasn't a big man, but nobody slept when he was on stage. He was near the bone, but he knew how to make you laugh. I remember seeing other big comedians at Blackpool, people like Tessie O'Shea and Sandy Powell, but there was nobody quite like Frank Randle.' Both Formby and Randle branched out into films, Randle all but doing it himself in a studio in a disused church in Manchester, and the same of course was true of another Blackpool favourite, Gracie Fields. There was scarcely a summer

Home-grown heroine: Gracie Fields in *Sally In Our Alley*.

in the 1930s when a Formby or Fields film was not to be seen at the resort's Princess cinema, and Gracie was also a regular live performer at the Grand. Holiday-makers at the Pleasure Beach in 1934 thought they were in heaven when they were allowed to glimpse her filming sequences for *Sing As You Go*.

In the 1950s, with Variety all washed up and sleazy 'tableaux' of scantily-clad girls doing nothing to stem the tide, the seaside was the last bastion of the good old all-action show with comics, singers, sand-dancers, conjurors and men who balanced girls in swimsuits on their noses. There could scarcely have been a better showcase for the comedians in the last wave of northern Variety, the likes of Ken Platt, Ken Dodd, Jewell and Warris, Morecambe and Wise, Al Read, Norman 'Over the Garden Wall' Evans, Sandy Powell, Hylda Baker and Ted Lune. Not all of them found the transition to the new world of television an easy one – even the peerless Doddy remains to this day essentially a stage performer – but here they could hone their craft on huge, responsive audiences of their kind of people, and they rewarded them with some memorable nights out. After them came shows headlined more

Blackpool legends: George Formby (above), Reginald Dixon and Charlie Cairoli (right).

often than not by the latest nine-day wonder at the top of the charts, unused to audiences bigger and older than those crushes of teenagers that crammed the cellar clubs of Liverpool or Manchester; but even then there was time for the likes of the young Les Dawson and Jimmy Tarbuck to taste the atmosphere of the big-time Variety stage, and both became more rounded (no reflection on their present-day physiques) performers for the experience. What times those were for catchphrases, too. Try to match the performers listed above with: 'Eeh, it's turned out nice again'; 'Eh, we've supped some stuff t'neet'; 'Hi'd like to say how tickled Hi ham – sex, missis, that's what they keep potatoes in in Lytham St Anne's'; 'Ah sed, Ah sed reet, Monkey'; 'She knows, y' know'; 'Can you 'ear me, mother?'

Tamer by far – and incomparably less pricy – than the glossy stage shows were the pierrots and concert parties, stemming unashamedly from the Victorian roots of black-faced minstrel shows and making no

The funny but not always funny-to-be-with Frank Randle. Some of the showgirls seem to be eyeing him with something less than adoration.

pretence at all of keeping abreast of the times. 'Corny' was the adjective most often applied to them, though usually in the most amiable of tones. '"My gosh, that was corny," my father would say when we came away from a concert party,' Michael Johns of Bury recalls. 'But as he said it the tears of laughter would be running down his cheeks, and he and my mother would be retelling gags and routines from the show for the rest of the week. I suppose they put 6d. in the hat to pay for all four of us, and I don't think you could say we didn't get our money's worth. It was

Pierrots on the sands at Filey, 1902, and a smartly turned-out Jumbles concert party.

the sheer awfulness of it all, of course, that was the real joke, dreadful comic cross-talk business that dragged on so long that in the end it just broke down your resistance. I remember that in Llandudno in the '50s the resident show at Happy Valley was headlined by Alex Munro, an old Scots comic best known to most of us south of the border as the father of the late actress Janet. I recall one particular routine by a Scots couple built up around the phrases:

'"Why was the hearse horse hoarse?"'

'"Because of the coffin."'

'Reference in the late 1950s to a hearse horse – or "Hersse horsse", as they pronounced it – probably tells you all you need to know about the age of this routine, but they milked it for all it was worth, minutes on end of it until you were beaten into surrender. Our other favourite concert party was the one on the front at Cleveleys, where you could always hear a good comic song. I don't know why, but I can remember at least two or three of them word-for-word almost to this day, which says a lot for the way they must have taught them to us on their big song-sheets. It also suggests we must have gone back to the show day after day, since I can't believe I could have absorbed all the lyrics to such little gems as *When I Was In The Services I Learned A Brand New Trade* or *How Much Salt Does A Salt Seller Sell When He Sells You A Cellar Full Of Salt?* at a single sitting.

'I think my favourite, though, to a jolly marching tune, was a song called *I Saw Esau*, which built considerably on the words of the old children's skipping chant. This went:

> I saw Esau sitting on a see-saw,
> I saw Esau with my girl,
> I saw Esau sitting on a see-saw,
> Giving her a merry whirl.
> I saw Esau, 'e saw me,
> I saw red and felt so sore,
> I got a saw, and I sawed Esau
> Off that old see-saw.

'Today, my children know the words to this song as well as I do, and it's such a daft little thing that I can't believe they won't be singing it to their children early in the next century. That's one wakes week memory that won't be dying with their old man. Other songs for the wakes weeks pandered unashamedly to the audience's Northern roots, and to

Dan Hardie's Players, Morecambe, 1911, and the Minstrels at Happy Valley, Llandudno, at much the same time.

the indomitable spirit in the face of adversity that both Lancastrians and Yorkshire folk like to see as part of their make-up. There was one that went:

> It'll be reet, it'll be reet,
> You sing it morning, afternoon and neet,
> Remember that in Lancasheer you sing with all your meet,
> It'll be reet, it'll be reet.

'I remember hearing that one at a concert party, almost certainly at Cleveleys, in the mid-'50s. And of course, songs like *Lassie From Lancashire* and *Ilkla Moor Baht 'At* would always be belted out with great gusto.'

Sally Robertson of Church is another with musical memories – cheap music, literally, but none the less evocative, to paraphrase Noel Coward. 'Whenever I think of Douglas, where a gang of six of us girls would go in Accrington wakes in around 1930, I remember the daytime sing-songs on the Prom,' she says. 'You'd be walking along and then all of a sudden there'd be a crowd of people all joining in with the latest songs, singing along to a piano and following the words on a screen with one of those ping-pong balls dancing along the lines. They'd be in a seafront building with a couple of shop fronts taken out, the kind they used for Dutch auctions, and rain or shine there'd always be a crowd. I remember joining in with some grand songs, novelty numbers like *Me And Jane In A Plane* and standards like *Red Sails In The Sunset*, and it was all free. The catch? Well, sheet music was the big thing in those days, with so many people having pianos, and at the end of the session fellers in straw hats and blazers would come round with great bundles of the songs under their arms trying to sell them. There was so much to do at Douglas, dancing at the Palace, which they used to say was the biggest ballroom in Europe, the Derby Castle, the Villa Marina or up at the camp for young men, Cunningham's, where they'd have lots of dances and the girls would float up in droves to fraternize with all the boys with their short back and sides. That's the way I remember them, anyway. I don't recall any rowdyism anywhere we went in Douglas, never anything other than people behaving themselves; there was certainly never any bother at Cunningham's Camp.'

J.B. Priestley was scathing about the song-pluggers in his classic book of social history, *English Journey*, based on his travels up and down the land in 1933. He particularly disliked their nasal accents, which was perhaps a reference to their attempts at an American twang but more likely, surely, to reflect the fact that after weeks on end in tennis bags and blazers in open-fronted shops at draughty seaside resorts the poor chaps were never without a streaming cold. Doris Smith of Whitefield, near Manchester, is another who remembers their efforts on the Isle of Man. 'It was a firm called Feldman's,' she recalls. 'They used to say that the pianist at Douglas was the sister of Florrie Ford, the old music hall star.' Mrs Smith also has fond memories of the dances at Cunningham's Camp: 'It was all part of the ritual; you'd have a good old sing for an hour at Feldman's, and then you'd go up to the dance at Cunningham's. The boys up there lived in either tents, chalets or flats, depending on what they could afford, and we always liked to pride ourselves on being able to tell who was staying where. I think the tents were pretty cheap, and the camp must have done a lot of good in giving a holiday to young men who wouldn't otherwise have had one. It seemed to be a fairly strict regime up there, and there was never any bother. But the dance hall was good, and it was always fun getting in in the first place. The camp was up a steep incline and you entered it via a chair lift, which was more like those contraptions old ladies use for getting upstairs at home than anything you'd see in the Alps. As we were all going up in our evening finery the lads from the camp would run down the slope weighing us all up, and if they saw anyone they fancied they'd do a sharp about turn and make themselves known.'

Light classical music was another wakes offering, particularly on Sunday nights, and the municipal theatres and holiday camps were especially strong on this. In a way it is no mystery; the BBC of Lord Reith's day was dominated by worthy music, the Sunday schools that most people attended at some stage of their life encouraged respect for tunes other than the latest Nat Gonella number, and the Northern brass band tradition meant that almost every field day, works gathering and League football match would be punctuated by the works of Sullivan or Offenbach. It was only when the Sunday school tradition waned that the singing of *Abide With Me* at the FA Cup Final degenerated from an intensely moving act of shared experience to a divisive, embarrassing shambles of obscenities being hurled from one end of Wembley Stadium to the other; that time, the early 1960s, coincided closely with the demise of the golden age of the wakes.

Of course, not every holiday-maker appreciated the joys of the palm court trio before a mid-evening nightcap of steaming Horlicks – 'Bit heavy-going, this, isn't it, luv?' – but Max Jaffa did not return to Scar-

borough and Bridlington for years on end for the good of his health, and
Butlin's decision to engage the San Carlo Opera Company in 1946 was
no mere gimmick; they certainly defended their decision vigorously
enough when middle-class critics who had hitherto been complaining
about their making life too easy for the jolly campers suddenly changed
tack and accused them of casting pearls before swine. Earlier this century,
before the First World War, Blackpool Winter Gardens had caused even
more of a sensation by engaging Enrico Caruso and Dame Nellie Melba
– and not to be outdone, in 1914 the Tower called in Dame Clara Butt to
rally patriotic fervour with her peerless *Land Of Hope And Glory* at a time
when its ballroom was being used for making silk parachutes. Needless
to say, the impresarios could have sold the tickets several times over, as
would most certainly be the case if they were to engage Luciano
Pavarotti or Dame Kiri Te Kanawa today. The Palace and Villa Marina
in Douglas were among other major halls that took pride in their high-
brow Sunday nights – and among the major coups of all time, the
Llandudno Pier Company raised eyebrows far and wide in 1926 by
hiring the brilliant young Malcolm Sargent to lick their orchestra into
shape. The later Sir Malcolm was always known for his streak of show-
manship, and more astringent critics used to sniff and call him Flash
Harry; needless to say, he made a splendid job of his relatively brief stay
beside the sea.

From such sublime heights it is a swoop indeed to the penny-in-the-
slot amusement arcades of the piers and promenades, but they are deep
in our wakes week folklore, too. 'You could certainly make a bob go
quite a long way,' Cec Hargreaves, brought up near Todmorden, recalls.
'When I was a teenager in the late '40s I loved those old machines. The
only ones you could gamble on were the big upright wooden cases with
the metal circular tracks behind glass. You'd press a lever to send the
ball spinning around a few times, at the end of which it would drop into
a cup marked 1d., 2d. or 3d. – or, far more likely, down to the hole at the
bottom which meant thank you very much, son, have another go.
Occasionally you'd hit the ball completely wrong and it would shoot
down into the reject hole on the first spin, as if it had been drawn down
by a magnet. But most of the time it would roll around the circle a few
times, so you had a second or two to dream that you might get 3d. out
of it at the end of your go. Some of them took ha'penny pieces, so you
were assured of twenty-four goes for a shilling, plus whatever you
picked up along the way.

'The other slot machines were pretty tawdry and pathetic. The peep-shows, the What The Butler Saw cards that you flicked through by turning a handle, were so old and decrepit by the '40s that they were just a laugh. But I hated those glass cases with scenes of haunted houses and hangings in them, where you put a penny in the slot to watch skeletons pop out of cupboards and convicts drop through trap doors. I just thought those were sick. I remember one particular one in Morecambe, the scruffiest thing you ever saw. It must have dated from the turn of the century, and it was so faded and thick with dust that you couldn't even tell the colour of the characters' clothes. I went on holiday in those days with a mate of mine called Vic, and when we went back the following year Vic said: "I wonder if they've still got that terrible old execution thing at the amusement arcade." When we got there we nearly died laughing. Most of it was as scruffy as before but all the characters, the convict, the gaoler, the priest and so on, had had new clothes knitted for them. Vic had an off-beat sense of humour and he just couldn't get over the thought of some woman solemnly sitting down somewhere in the middle of winter in Morecambe knitting clothes for miniature convicts and gaolers. The convict's grey suit even had little black arrows sewn on in cotton, and it just slayed Vic to think that somebody could lavish such detail on something so tatty and useless and nasty. Years later I saw him in the street, not long before he died, and before I even recognized him he shouted:

'"Hey-up, Cec, what about them little arrows at Morecambe, then?"'

Michael Johns of Bury says that he was a great scavenger around the arcades, a snapper-up of the occasional unconsidered trifle in the form of uncollected winnings in the little bronze semicircular pots at the bottom of the machines: 'I'd scour those places for lost pennies. To me it was better fun, a more entertaining gamble, than playing the machines – and most of the time a more profitable one, too. But even looking for money wasn't a casino where you couldn't lose. You only had to let a penny slip from your hand and it was odds-on that it would make a bee-line for a crack between the pier boards and plunge down into the murky waters or the puddly beach below. If it was water, well, you'd had it. But I remember agonising long and hard, once, over whether to pursue a penny I dropped down through the boards on to the sand before persuading myself just to put it down to experience. After an evening of foraging for pennies, though, I'd often go back to the digs and dream all night about finding perhaps sixpence in one winnings cup, and eightpence in the next, and so on. And I remember to this day the day after Southport Pier burned down in 1959. My dad read out a newspaper report saying that all the machines had plunged down to the beach and spilled their contents, and people had been down there picking up still-warm pennies from the sands. I was aged about 13 and at the height of my scavenging career, and I remember thinking that I'd have given anything to have been the first and only person under Southport Pier that evening, gathering warm pennies as the firemen doused the smouldering remains above.'

Amid the amusement arcades, tea rooms, palmists' booths and shellfish and fish and chip stalls of the pre-war seafronts would be freak shows that revolted passers-by even then – and revolt the memory and the imagination even more today. That having been said, nobody ever starved running a freak show in an English seaside resort in the 1920s and '30s – and some, like the Blackpool showman Luke Gannon, did very nicely indeed. A Burnley man in his middle years and married to a palmist and clairvoyant called Madame Kusharney, he had a long and tawdry record as a huckster and tipster behind him when he hit gold in the 1930s. The brainwave for which he is still known to this day, the subject of at least one play and a string of television documentaries over the years, was his exhibiting of the Rector of Stiffkey on the Golden Mile. But that was only the tip of a grubby iceberg.

The poor old Rector of Stiffkey, from a hitherto blameless and remote spot pronounced Stewkey by its natives and lying up on the north coast of Norfolk east of the Wash, had been turfed out of the Church of England in 1932 for alleged misbehaviour with troubled young women whose souls he was meant to be saving. Rumour had it that Gannon offered him £100 a week to assuage his guilt on the Golden Mile and the man of the cloth succumbed to temptation once again, saying he needed the money to appeal against the Church court's judgement. After that he submitted himself to humiliations almost beyond belief. He lived in a barrel on the Golden Mile alongside Gannon's other big attraction of the time, a girl called Barbara Cockayne who was fasting for a fortnight in this world of fish and chip fumes and the sharp tang of vinegared shrimps; posters announcing that the Rector would watch over Barbara apparently horrified the confused clergyman. Next it was his turn to fast, in a glass case, and as a *coup de grâce* he was to be seen in the fake flames of Hell being prodded by forks. 'Have You Seen Poor Old Stiffkey, The Lad From The Village?' read signposts along the Mile, accompanied by a picture of a silly looking parson. After this, his penance presumably paid, he turned his back on Blackpool and returned to the east coast, where he appeared as a saintly soul akin to

Daniel in the Lion's Den at a sideshow in Skegness. Once again, however, his judgement was called into doubt – this time with fatal consequences. The point about Daniel was that his previous pious conduct stood him in good stead against the savage beasts; but the lions of Skegness obviously knew a thing or two about the Rector of Stiffkey's murky history over on the other side of the Wash, and gave him a mauling from which he died in August, 1938. This was all some hundreds of miles from Luke Gannon's Blackpool booth, of course, but the old showman paid tasteful tribute to his former star by fishing his barrel out of storage, laying a plank across it and placing atop it all a sheet-covered sack arranged to look like a human body. As this was a gesture being made with selfless sincerity, there was no day-glo poster suggesting what might have been under the sheet, and Mr Gannon was doubtless horrified when large numbers of people of morbid taste were drawn towards his booth at the sight of it. 'Look, Bill, the body's in the bag,' a social researcher employed by Mass-Observation overheard one passer-by remark; surely not the reaction that was in the grief-stricken Luke Gannon's mind?

The day-glo posters they did see at his stall that summer of 1938 are also recalled by tens of thousands of visitors to Blackpool in those last summers before the Second World War:

On A Strange Honeymoon
Love Calling
Colonel Barker
Admission Twopence
Colonel Barker And His Or Her Bride
How Long Can A Loving Couple Remain
Under These Conditions?

The rather confused yarn was that the Colonel, born a woman, had undertaken the world's first sex change operation. He had then married as a man – but since the law did and indeed still does not recognize sex changes, the union was unique in the world as a marriage of two women. The reason the two were lying in separate beds with thousands of people traipsing around them at 2d. a time every day was down to a bet made by the Colonel – allegedly of £250 – to the effect that he would find the willpower to resist putting his manhood to the test for twenty-one weeks. This was presumably no problem during 'working' hours – 'He's getting some bloody easy money,' one punter was heard to mut-

ter, gazing down at the newspapers, cheap novels and Craven A
cigarettes surrounding the contented looking couple in their respective
beds – while at night they were watched over every second by trained
and vigilant staff.

The truth of the case, of course, was very different. The Colonel was a
conman who got up every evening after the hordes had left and went
back to the lodgings he shared with somebody else's wife; his virgin
bride Eva, who had first come to Blackpool to do a starving newlyweds
act with one Spud Murphy  – 'Two Genuine Little Love Birds Straight
From The Altar . . . What An Awful Queer Honeymoon' – toddled off to
her own digs until the morrow. The following morning they would be
back for another day in bed, and the crowds would again come flocking.
According to Mass-Observation, thousands an hour would visit them on
a good day, peering down at 'two ordinary, pleasant looking people in
bed, in no way exhibiting their bodies.' The researchers felt that the
scene somehow symbolized the Blackpool of the late 1930s – a lot of
thinking about sex, but not much action. Doubtless not every visitor
made that connection.

Happily, Luke Gannon was foiled in what would doubtless have been
his finest hour, but at least he could not be accused of not trying. In
August 1935, on reading that the Queen of Abyssinia had completed a
sixteen-day religious fast as a protest against war, he cabled her as one
pioneer of pacifism to another suggesting that she should repeat the
exercise immediately at Blackpool, 'which for the next eight weeks is a
visiting centre for tourists from all over the world'. He claimed he had
already suggested that the town should stage a Pageant of World's
Peace, and in a later letter he explained that he believed her visit would
'cement by sympathetic understanding of the simple-minded, sincere
people of good will . . . that universal brotherhood by which alone can
any lasting peace be secured'. It was a fact that Gannon had suggested
to the Blackpool town fathers in the previous year that a Grand
Spectacular Pageant should be staged but, oddly, any mention of world
peace seemed to have slipped his mind when laying out his proposals,
the only apparent motive being an earlier start to the tourist season.
Whatever, the Blackpool authorities did not want to know about it –
which meant that the Queen of Abyssinia never did come and starve in
one of Luke Gannon's barrels and help him uphold his claim to a Mass-
Observation researcher that 'You can divide the public like this: 50 per
cent certifiable, 30 per cent on the brink and the other 20 per cent living
on the others.'

Another grand old seaside institution, the comic postcard, was a further eye-catcher among the Promenade booths and stalls. Picture postcards stemmed from 1894, when it became legal to send them through the post for half the normal rate, a halfpenny, without an envelope. The big breakthrough came eight years later, in 1902, when the Post Office allowed messages as well as the address to be written on them, and from that day the century's first big collecting craze was born. Early saucy cards did not run much beyond drawings of pretty girls tumbling and showing a leg – but by the time of the wakes' golden years events had progressed apace, and the efforts of the artist Donald McGill and the Holmfirth publishers Bamforth are deep in the lore of all who have browsed through the seafront carousel racks and spun them round quickly to sunset scenes across the bay at the sight of Great Aunt Maud coming round the corner. From the earliest days there was a brisk trade in cards aimed at working people rejoicing over their freedom from the factory or mill for the week; there was a particularly vivid and earthy series celebrating the weavers' lot on holiday. Later, in the McGill era and into the 1950s, a steady seller was always an entirely innocent picture of a working lass lazing in a deckchair and saying how good it was to forget it all, while a variation for men was what the Yorkshire writer Maurice Colbeck describes as 'a plethora of impossibly foaming tankards usually accompanied by huge plates of fish and chips; the idea was, presumably, that the Northerner on holiday would send these home in the certain knowledge that they would reduce his work-bound colleagues to frenzied envy.' In truth, you could not go very far wrong with cards like these – but there lay snares and pitfalls in other comic classics.

'I blame a dirty postcard for losing me a girl who would almost certainly have become my wife,' says Ged Armfield, who was brought up in Bradford. 'I'd been courting her for nine months or so when I went on holiday with a gang of pals to Bridlington in 1934. I sent her a postcard home every day, sea views and sunsets and what-not until on the fourth day I sent her one of a girl walking along the Prom. The only reason I sent it was that this girl honestly reminded me of her, with a nice big toothy smile and dark brown wavy hair. She was carrying an umbrella, and the caption was something about it being showery and her having had it up and down all week. My relationship with my girlfriend was not sexual in the way you'd use the term today; after all, we'd been courting for less than a year, and that was seen as nothing in those days. But we were pretty close, and I thought that was just about the kind of joke I could get away with with her – which it might have been on the back row of the one-and-nines after a couple of drinks on a Saturday night. The only trouble was, the first she saw of it was at half past seven on a Thursday morning at the breakfast table, with her mam and dad looking over her shoulder. Well, there was a hell of a row when I got back, and that was that. I'll never know whether she was really embarrassed, or whether she was just putting on a show for her parents. I've often wished I'd gone back to find out, to see if it was all an act. We'd got on so well up until then, very close and happy. But she never made any effort to see me, either, after that, so perhaps it really was the end of the road and I'd misread her. I comfort myself by thinking that if I'd misread her on that issue it wouldn't have been long before I misread her on something else, and so perhaps we weren't so compatible after all. But it still upsets me to think that the decision was taken out of my hands by that damned postcard.'

Perhaps Ged Armfield would have benefited from greater vigilance by the resort's watch committee, an institution that became famous as a guardian of public decency in the golden years, scrutinizing each proposed comic card as it came in from the publishers. Not surprisingly, Blackpool's censors were more high-profile than most, and details have emerged over the years of several Bamforth cards they turned down, at least at the first time of asking. They include such gems as:

'Wife: "Why Don't You Bite My Ear In Bed Like You Used To?"

Husband: "I Can't. My Teeth Are In The Bathroom."'

Then there was the one of the short-sighted visitor saying 'I See He Has His Mother's Rosy Cheeks' at the sight of a baby in his birthday suit lying across his mum's knee. And who can ever forget that deathless exchange, most certainly accepted by later censorship committees, in which the perennial doctor and patient are face to face:

'Doctor: "You've Got Stomach Trouble. You'll Have To Diet."

Patient: "What Colour?"'

They don't write them like that any more. But at least they keep on trying.

# CHAPTER 6

# *All For Your Delight*

It was rather posh going to Butlin's in the early years. In 1946 you were definitely doing all right if you aspired to a week in your own self-contained chalet, waited on hand and foot by Redcoats and less glamorous menials, at £6 16s. 6d. each a week and half price for the kids. You had to work some overtime to be thinking along those kind of lines, with the rail fare on top. In fact most happy campers were lower to middle management types, characterized in those days as clerical workers. The only family on our street that managed a week at Prestatyn was headed by a man who sold insurance for the Pru.

Holiday camps had started in the 1930s as part of a coming together of a variety of inter-war fads and trends, most of them associated with greater mobility and awareness of the world beyond the town boundaries. People in Britain had been a sociable bunch throughout late Victorian and Edwardian times, loving their music halls, bars, outings, and Sunday evening 'monkey runs', the weekly get-togethers at which youngsters would eye each other up and sometimes get up to rather more besides after the crowds had dispersed. After the First World War cheap travel by bus and train and all the latest music from the London hot spots on the wireless opened up new vistas by both day and night, and by the 1930s dance halls, cinemas, big roadside pubs, motor racing circuits and out-of-town lido pools were heralding an exciting new world of art deco concrete and glass that was suddenly accessible to millions. Coupled with this was a cult for the Great Outdoors – for hiking and biking, tennis and tugs-o'-war – a movement which owed at least something to the early 1930s' constant newsreel reports of clean-limbed and lithe young Germans having sun-blessed fun in the Black Forest, years before real alarm about their Nazi leaders' motives set in. It was

71

quite a heady mixture, the physical contact of the crowded bar and dance floor, the healthy glow of fit and tanned bodies, the feeling of being in on something big and new and exciting, that had the likes of the young poetic 'toff' John Betjeman looking in from the outside on a brave new world in which the traditional privileged classes played no part. They could keep their marble halls. The concrete and glass halls were the ones everyone was talking about, and if you had a regular job on decent pay they were open to you, no questions asked; this was the age in which the holiday camps were born.

Billy Butlin was the king, of course. He had been in on the first wave in the late '30s at Skegness and Clacton, and come the 1950s he was a household name, a post-war superstar ranking alongside Lady Docker, Len Hutton, Stanley Matthews, Alma Cogan and the Comet airliner in terms of column inches written about him in the *Mail, Sketch* and *News Chronicle*. A genial travelling showman from South Africa via Canada, he had rested his caravan and little funfair of half a dozen attractions in Skegness in 1927, adding a scenic railway and dodgems the following year. It was the dodgems that did it. Bought for £2,000, including a bor-

A message – and an institution – that passed into holiday legend: Butlin's first camp at Skegness, opened in 1936.

rowed £200, they were a huge hit, and Butlin had no hesitation in snapping up the sole agency for selling them in Europe when it came along. 'The dodgems were a major turning point in my life,' he later recalled. 'With their success I came into the really big money. I was on the way towards realizing the holiday camp dream.' His first move was to open up a string of six other amusement parks in the south-east; but he stayed with Skegness for the Big One, and after an investment of £50,000 the first Butlin's camp opened to 500 holiday-makers on Easter Saturday, 1936. Early newspaper advertisements pictured an old-style showman beating a drum, for Butlin was never a man for complicated messages. The words were pretty persuasive, too: 'The most modern Camp in the world, with all the amenities of a first-class Hotel. FREE Golf, Tennis, Bathing, Bowls, Dancing and Concert Parties, Boating and Licensed Club. FOUR good meals a day, cooked by experienced chefs in hygienic kitchens. Cosy Elizabethan Chalets with electric light, carpeted floors, running water, baths and first-class sanitary arrangements – ALL FOR £2 5s. PER WEEK.'

Not surprisingly, he was doing well enough before the war, but by the summer of 1946 he simply could not open new camps quickly enough. There was an old joke told by Variety comedians about the Second World War having been started by Dame Vera Lynn's agent; by that reckoning, the suspicion must remain that the fighting was ended by Butlin's bank manager, for while the White Cliffs Of Dover songbird won the war, Billy most certainly won the peace. One would have thought that after six years of communal living and getting fell in, Britain's returning soldiers, sailors and airmen would have wanted nothing more than a holiday away from it all with their families. Instead, the cheerful team spirit that helped Britons through the hard times both abroad and on the home front spilled over joyously for a few years into civilian life, and nothing captured its essence better than the holiday camps. By accident or design, Butlin and his imitators struck upon an almost perfect formula for combining the kind of disciplined living needed to feed, say, 5,000 campers at Filey or Skegness four times a day, with a lively and almost self-parodying sense of fun.

'I think too much has been made of the regimented side of holiday camps,' says Ted Barrett of Leeds. 'I'd served in France after D-Day and I can tell you, there was not a lot of comparison between Normandy in the summer of 1944 and Butlin's at Skegness in the summer of 1947. It's nicer to get up to a record blaring:

Roll out of bed in the morning,
With a great big smile and a good, good morning,
Get up with a grin,
There's a good day tumbling in!
Wake with the sun and the rooster,
Cock-a-doodle-do like the rooster use'ter,
How can you go wrong
If you roll out of bed with a song?

than to some fool playing Reveille. And if you just turned over and
didn't get up, so what? You missed your breakfast, but there was no
Sergeant Major to hammer in and tip you out of bed. It was the same
with that old business of splitting the campers up into houses, cheering
on our team mates. It was fun for the little kids, but after all we'd been
through, do you think that any of us adults gave a toss whether the
Knobbly Knees winner came from Gloucester house or the Glamorous
Granny from Kent? I'd say it was because we'd had to lead such a disciplined life over the previous years that this cod regimentation at Butlin's
was such a big hit. It was just playing at being ordered about as far as
we were concerned, a send-up of the life we'd been living where at the
end of the day you could just tell the "officers" – the Redcoats – to get
stuffed. I think Butlin's recognized this pretty well. The head lad on site
was called the Camp Commandant, and I think they might have done
something about that earlier if they could live their time over again, but
all the games and contests were very light and low-key. Oh, yes, Butlin's
was one up on the army, I can tell you.'

Ted Barrett's recollections seem to be echoed by a 1946 advertising
campaign for one of Butlin's big camps in North Wales, always a major
draw for the wakes towns: 'Don't - please don't – get the idea that
you've GOT TO BE GAY at Prestatyn. You can take part in the fun or if
you choose be a spectator – whichever attracts you. No compulsion. No
chivvying you to do this or that. Nor should there be; you are the guest
– and it's your holiday!' That having been said, the herd instinct was
never greater in Britain than in those immediate post-war years, and
while the nation shocked and baffled the world by rejecting its war-time
hero Churchill in the 1945 general election, it was more predictable and
conservative in flocking back in record numbers to all the old and com-
fortingly familiar pleasures of the soccer stadium, cinema and speedway
track. So many attendance records at Northern football grounds were
set at that time: 78,000 at Goodison Park for the Everton-Liverpool

derby of 1948-9; 36,000 at the Shay for Halifax's cup tie with Spurs in '52-3; 61,000 at Anfield for the Liverpool-Wolves cup game of '51-2; 24,000 at little Spotland for another cup tie, Rochdale v Notts County, in '49-50; 25,000 for two games at Rotherham in 1952; 27,000 at Stockport's Edgeley Park for Liverpool's cup visit in '49-50; and frequently massive crowds on the great open terraces of Maine Road, Burnden Park, Elland Road, Deepdale and their like. Yes, we liked one another's company in the years immediately after the war, and while, to quote the now quaintly archaic words of the Butlin's brochure, the campers did not have to feel they had GOT TO BE GAY, by far the majority of them were more than happy to be so.

Everyone was talking about holiday camps in the late 1940s, and at any sign of interest slackening, Billy would come up with some new idea to put them to the fore again. There were big off-season reunions of the Butlin's Physical Recreation and Social Club in Manchester and other major centres, where the happy campers of the summer could sip sherry, renew friendships, look back on jolly times by the pool or on the dance floor – and lay down plans for more of the same next August; every year a special badge would be struck for junior campers, Skegness 1955 or whatever, and even small gestures like these would help create a sense of place and occasion. And to counteract the accusation that entertainment did not stray beyond sports, dancing and funfair rides, Butlin's camps always took delight in confounding their critics by interspersing their programmes with debates, brains trusts, and for one astounding short season in 1946 – as mentioned above – concerts by the San Carlo Opera Company. Even before the war they had gone for the big names in light entertainment, among them Gracie Fields, George Robey, Elsie and Doris Waters and Vic Oliver. And much later, in 1961, the creator of Billy Bunter, Frank Richards, was commissioned to write a book about the Fat Owl and his chums' stay at a Butlin's camp. Not surprisingly, the big oaf did not take kindly to the morning risings: 'I'm not turning out yet!' he yapped. 'We're on holiday, ain't we? Think I'm going to turn out as if we were at school? What's the good of a holiday if a fellow can't have his sleep out? Go and eat coke.'

By no means everything said about the eventual Sir Billy's ventures was kind. As one of the first major social trends of the post-war years, holiday camps were debated endlessly in the press and on radio, and the forces of intellectual snobbery soon began to line up against them when their appeal widened down-market, fulminating against holiday-makers too lazy to organize their own entertainment. All too often the theme was taken up by working people who secretly would have been more than happy to enjoy such privileges had they been able to afford to do so, but who instead tried to make a virtue of being 'independent', staying in digs and making their own way. What irritated a lot of those on the outside looking in was the seemingly ever-open doors of the holiday camp bars, unrestrained as private establishments by the tough licensing laws of the day. Class prejudice again seemed to play a part in this; so long as the camp bars attracted a 'golf club' type of clientele their day-long opening prompted little comment; but when working people moved in, their access to such joys was instantly questioned.

'I never remember any bother with drink in the years we went to holiday camps,' says Ted Barrett. 'It seemed to me that they made the bars deliberately lively with singing and music, presumably to sell more ale, so they could hardly complain, and to be fair they didn't complain if things got a bit noisy at half past ten on a Saturday night. But the fact was that most of us were there on a fixed budget, with our money for the week stashed safely away somewhere or even sewn into our vests. Those were the days before cash dispensers, credit cards or even bank accounts, unless you were very lah-de-dah, so if you ran out of money on Thursday there were no "extras" at the camp for you for the rest of the week. You just lived on what you'd already paid for, which was quite enough to survive on but not much fun without the odd pint of wallop to wash it down, or an ice cream for the kids. That's what really made those holiday camps so dear, the bars and snack bars everywhere. But as I say, money was pretty tight all round, so the fact that in theory you could have been drinking from soon after breakfast to bedtime didn't mean that that was what you were doing.'

Along with the myths about drink were lurid tales of holiday camps being dens of vice. Ted Barrett, a young father at the time of his visits in the late 1940s, is sceptical. 'There was always this risqué image bubbling under the surface, but it was more in people's minds than anything else,' he suggests. 'I suppose it was something to do with the drinking, the dancing, the keep-fit regimes and the absence of nosy landladies. But you couldn't get up to very much in those chalets without the rest of the row knowing about it, and besides, most of the campers in my experience were young couples with families rather than single people on the lookout for action. It always struck me that it was the Redcoats who had most of the fun as far as that kind of thing was concerned, especially some of the more senior men. They did tend to be single people, bright and outgoing and with the opportunity to get to know the young women under their command over several weeks. It's often been said that some of them took advantage of that. There were some real cases among the staff, I can tell you. Lots of comedians and entertainers started out as Redcoats, of course – Des O'Connor, Dave Allen, Roy Hudd, Jimmy Tarbuck, Charlie Drake – and it's often part of their routine to joke about all the sexy goings-on at holiday camps. I think they must have helped to fuel the myth, over the years – unless everyone else was having a ball, unbeknown to me, and I was the only one missing out!'

Most people who remember Butlin's from the 1950s swear that nobody ever shouted 'Hi-de-hi' and insisted on a return yell of 'Ho-de-ho' in their presence, but in a book published in 1947 the social historian J.A.R. Pimlott recorded that it happened at at least one camp during meal times. What comes through most strongly of all, however, is just how far ahead of its time the Butlin organisation was, and how innovations introduced just before or after the war are still seen as cornerstones of good public relations today. There was the relaxed informality of calling the lavatories 'Lads' and 'Lasses' – twee and irksome to some, but almost revolutionary in an age when public notices were taken very seriously, and you could not go over a level crossing without passing a sign telling you in hundreds of words the whys and wherefores of who was responsible for what. The public address system, Radio Butlin, anticipated community and local radio in this country by decades, and the *Butlin Times* was an in-house newspaper of the kind to which some quite progressive companies are still only just coming around in the 1990s. As for corporate identity, still a buzz-word today, what could have been more simple and economical than dressing the more high-profile staff in a job lot of red jackets?

Strictly in the cause of research, Pimlott spent a day at one of the big Butlin camps in August, 1946, very much in the spirit of the Mass-Observation team in Blackpool a few years earlier. While somehow managing to maintain the researcher's almost obligatory stance of intellectual superiority – mainly because the whole exercise, when you come to think about it, is rather akin to visiting a human zoo – the general impression is that he was pleasantly surprised in some respects and impressed throughout by Butlin's organizational skills. Of the midday meal he wrote: 'Lunch was an impressive demonstration of efficiency. . . . The service was speedy and the food was good. Soup, meat pie and vegetables, steamed pudding, it was a mass-produced meal but substantial and well enough prepared. No bread – owing to rationing. Tea to drink afterwards, and I was told that tea is served at every meal.' And of the campers: 'The company looked unremarkable – a good solid mixture of respectable people of all ages, with none of the ostentatious jollity of which I had read – at a guess clerical workers, shop assistants and similar folk. Few of them were in holiday attire, still fewer could be said to be smartly dressed, and the general impression was rather drab.' It seems almost with an air of regret that Pimlott records that 'there were no "Hi-de-hi's" and "Ho-de-ho's".'

For many men who were young adults in the war years, the chief memory of Butlin's camps is not of family holidays but of basic armed services training before being posted abroad. Philip Bollom, who went on to become a dry cleaning magnate with the Bootle-based Johnson Group, remembered for the rest of his life his initiation into the Royal Navy at the Skegness camp in 1944. 'Emblazoned across the wall was the motto "Our True Intent Is All For Your Delight",' he recalled shortly before his death in 1990. 'At the time it seemed that the camp's temporary proprietors might have tried a bit harder to live up to it.' Butlin's started in the South, but their rapid expansion to Northern resorts made them a magnet for wakes holidaymakers. Today the company concentrates its activities on five huge Holiday Worlds, including Starcoast at Pwllheli and Funcoast at its original Skegness stamping ground. But it also owns traditional seafront hotels in five resorts, big pleasure palaces that it has refurbished to appeal to mature couples; and as these include the Metropole in Blackpool and the Grands in Scarborough and Llandudno, it is plain that the North is still at the heart of its thinking.

# CHAPTER 7

# *Boots And Bags And Cheerful Chatter*

*I'm Happy When I'm Hiking*, the song went, and its jolly all-join-together tune encapsulated one of the great crazes of the inter-war years. Cycling was another, though it was never quite so popular, perhaps because it was slightly less sociable; even on the roads of the 1920s and early '30s it was rather less easy to meander along on bikes swapping stories and

The joys of camping, 1907.

telling jokes than it was on foot on the heights of North Wales or the Lake District, and cycling also tended to highlight the gulf in physical strength more starkly than an amiable ramble. In any walking party there were always the speed merchants, almost all of them fit young men of about 20; but after that you would have the main pack and then the stragglers, both of them groups of mixed sex with lots to talk about, and quips and sandwiches to be shared. In cycling in those days of the big, heavy touring bike, the first steep upward hill sorted the boys from the girls on grounds of sheer brute force, and that was the way it would stay for the rest of the spin. The result was that unless you invested in a tandem, bikes became more of a male preoccupation – and more competitive, too. It is no surprise that Reg Harris, Britain's most celebrated cyclist of all time, was a Bury lad who performed some of his greatest feats at a Northern track, Fallowfield in South Manchester. It is only in this last generation that the cry 'Oo do you think you are, then, Reg

Off for a spin, 1929.

'Arris?' has ceased to go up behind some suburban speedster who has whizzed past a more plodding pedaller.

The hiking craze was nationwide, and it was reflected in silly songs on the radio, Variety sketches – Frank Randle was never happier than in his daft khaki shorts – and advertising. You could buy Hikers Pic-Nic biscuits by Barratt's at two for a penny; 'Hikey! That's Shell – that was!' gasped an impressed walker, rucksack on back, in the petrol company's famous 'double-headed' campaign of the 1930s. A considerable cottage industry, in most cases a literal description, sprang up among families offering bed and breakfast to walkers and cyclists in country areas that had not previously suspected that they had charms to attract tourists, and new life came to tired old health spas such as Buxton, where a dwindling guest list of the infirm and elderly was suddenly boosted by the pink-cheeked hordes from off the tops. What did it matter that big, muddy boots were not always compatible with parquet floors?

For all its universal appeal, hiking was nowhere more popular than in the mill towns and big cities of the North. Part of the reason was purely geographical, with the Lake and Peak Districts and the Yorkshire Dales on the doorstep; part of it was practical, as nowhere else in the length and breadth of England did so many people live so unremittingly in smoke and grime, or feel a greater need to get away from it all as education gave them clearer insights into the effects of such filth on their health. But there was more to it than that, and it was bound up with concepts that extended rather beyond the mill gates – disenchantment with the Establishment after the disaster of the First World War, the rise of socialist politics in the Depression and a new-found awareness of the rights - or at least the justifiable claims – of working men. As hiking grew in popularity, more and more people began to question why so many of the open moorlands that surrounded their home towns were inaccessible. In the feverish years of the Depression that saw the Labour Party progress from recognition as the official Opposition in 1922 to Government two years later, there was no shortage of young men to stand up and explain to their fellow workers that it was only in the early nineteenth century that the ruling classes had robbed the public of a vast network of ancient moorland tracks, enclosing them and protecting them with gamekeepers in defence of their selfish interest in shooting grouse. From then on, small groups of enthusiasts took to the hills whenever possible, not simply for the good of their health but deliberately to flout the law and exert what they saw as their age-old rights to wander the paths of their forefathers. Like any successful civic rights

campaign it was a heady mixture of idealism, camaraderie, good fun –
and the invigorating and sustaining feeling that you knew, deep down,
that you were right.

The climax of their campaign came in April 1932, when a mass trespass on Kinder Scout in the Peak District by between 400 and 600 walkers resulted in scuffles to disarm gamekeepers of their sticks, in which
one of them twisted an ankle, and the arrest of six of the protesters.
'When the Manchester contingent returned to Hayfield, six of us were
arrested and kept overnight,' Benny Rothman, one of the men who in
this age of instant labels would doubtless be known as the Kinder Scout
Six, recalls. 'We were subsequently brought to trial by magistrates in
New Mills and after a number of court appearances were finally
brought to trial by jury at Derby Assizes. There we faced a remarkable
group of jurors including two brigadier generals, three colonels, two
captains and two majors, most of whom were landowners. Needless to
say, we were found guilty and sentenced to prison terms ranging from
two to six months. I got five months.' The trespass was organized by the
left-wing  British Workers' Sports Federation, and many of the established rambling groups that opposed it as counter-productive at the
time joined together into the Ramblers' Association in 1935 to lobby in
more conventional ways. The access lobby's position was summed up
by another prominent campaigner, P.A. Barnes of Sheffield:

> Although Bleaklow is only sixteen miles in a straight line from the
> centres of either Manchester or Sheffield, there are surrounding this
> ridge thirty-seven square miles of wild country quite unknown except
> to the few ramblers who defy these unjust restrictions and take the
> access so far denied to them by the law. Similarly, to the east of the
> Derwent reservoirs there are the extensive Broomhead, Howden and
> Derwent moorlands, in all covering thirty-two square miles, with only
> three undisputed public ways across them, while Kinder Scout, af-
> fording in many ways the most exhilarating and picturesque scenery
> in the district, is very strictly preserved. Here are fifteen square miles
> of mountainous country with no public path. . . . Through the moor-
> land area in or adjacent to the Peak District, about 215 square miles,
> there are only twelve footpaths across moorland that exceed two
> miles in length. The rest are mainly short paths near the fringe of the
> moors.

The campaigners did well to concentrate their efforts on the breathtaking Kinder Scout, which had the advantages of a memorable name and a distinct peak with which people could identify, the kind of noble summit that would have looked well on T-shirts and badges in a later age of lobbying. Like the Devil, these earnest law-breakers even had the best tunes, or one of them, anyway, in the Salford teenager Ewan MacColl's *Manchester Rambler*, with its chorus extolling the rights of the Monday morning wage slave to be the Sunday free man. MacColl, who was press officer for the 1932 mass trespass, wrote more commercial songs in *Dirty Old Town* and *The First Time Ever I Saw Your Face*, the latter of which became an international hit when recorded by the American superstar Roberta Flack; but none means more to a group of ageing Lancastrians than his battle hymn for the freedom to walk the tops, even though their campaign led only to the 1939 Access to Mountains Act, which in its final corrupted form read more like a grouse moor owners' charter, and later to the still unsatisfactory National Parks and Access to the Countryside Act of 1949.

As a result, the fight continues to this day, and those familiar with the inner workings of the Ramblers' Association still see divisions in the ranks between a Northern membership that stays committed to putting access to open moorland at the top of the agenda and Southern members more concerned with farmland footpaths. That, however, did not prevent the Ramblers from organizing a rally to commemorate the sixtieth anniversary of the mass trespass in April, 1992, an event for which Mike Harding wrote a play, *A Free Man On Sunday*, and at which Ewan MacColl's widow Peggy Seeger joined others in singing his *Manchester Rambler*. At the same time the Ramblers' Association president Chris Hall took the opportunity to endorse the mass trespass, which captured the imagination of so many Lancashire and Yorkshire mill town lads and lasses, when he wrote:

> In 1932 there was no Ramblers' Association. The ramblers' federations of the day stood aside from the trespass, indeed some denounced it, lest it prejudiced their own 'constitutional' campaign for the grant of access to the hills. With hindsight we can see how wrong they were. The trespass, by demonstrating the depths of ramblers' anger and the selfish over-reaction of the landowners, gave a powerful forward thrust to the campaign which eventually won the (sadly flawed) National Parks and Access to the Countryside Act of 1949. . . . The clear lesson of 1932 – and all that has happened since – is that landowners, with very few shining exceptions, will not concede rights

The great Kinder mass trespass story of 1932, taking precedence on the *Daily Dispatch's* front page over a Hitler election triumph and the 'over-the-line' FA Cup Final, in which Newcastle beat Arsenal with the help of one of the most controversial goals in football history.

of access unless compelled to do so by articulate, resolute, organized public opinion.

Joan McKichan of Aberdeen, who started rambling the Peak District towards the end of the golden age of the wakes in the late 1950s, recalls that there was still an underlying consciousness of those battles of a generation earlier, still a distance between the 'official' Ramblers and the Manchester trespassers. 'The train from London Road station would be packed, and the atmosphere was very different from what you'd find on a trip to the seaside,' she says. 'There was a great deal of pride and dedication involved, more than you might naturally expect to be inspired by

Manchester girls in the Peak District, 1961.

the simple pursuit of walking sometimes hard but almost never danger-
ous moorland paths with a group of friends and acquaintances. I know
the National Parks Act left so many loopholes that must be filled, but it
certainly succeeded in making the Kinder Scout area more open to all
human life. One time around 1960 I came across a group of young
prisoners out on a walk, with pairs of them linked by chain and another
chain the length of their file, and that was a depressing sight. Another
day, dropping down through the mists, we came over the brow of a
ridge and saw a group of white-robed figures dancing in a circle.
Perhaps they were Druids, but at the time they struck me more as members of the Ku-Klux-Klan; we didn't stop to ask, anyway. It probably
sounds sacrilegious to the ears of the Manchester Ramblers, but those
were two occasions when I would have settled for rather less public
access to the hills. . . .'

Joan McKichan was first drawn to hiking in the 1950s by the high-profile advertising of Sunday morning excursions to Derbyshire from Manchester London Road station, later renamed Piccadilly. Since most
walkers from the mill towns arrived at Victoria, on the other side of

town, central Manchester at around 8 a.m. on dry summer Sundays would be thronging with hearty souls in big boots and what were yet to become widely known as anoraks – 'windjammers' was the more down-to-earth term – trekking intrepidly up Cannon or Market Street. Once at London Road there would be similar crowds from every other corner of Manchester, and Mrs McKichan recalls that on busy days, besides those who wished to strike off on their own, there would be groups for up to six different walks, ranging from A through B1, B2, B3 and B4 to C. She even wrote a poem, *Sunday Excursion,* published in the *Ramblers' Magazine* of the day. 'It's no work of Shakespeare, but it brings back something of the time and the people,' she says.

> Train's full.
> Full of what?
> Boots and bags and cheerful chatter.
> Train moves.
> Moves where?
> From the station with a clatter.
>
> 'Here's a crossword!'
> 'Seen *The Climber*?'
> 'Who's got this month's *Ramblers' Mag?*'
> 'Hey, mate, this is a No Smoker,
> Here's the guard,
> Put out your fag.'
>
> Train stops.
> Stops where?
> In the country where it's quiet.
> Out jump
> Ramblers.
> And the platform's in a riot.
>
> 'Where's my ticket?'
> 'Where's my map gone?'
> 'Where's the leader for B2?'
> 'Someone said it's 18 miles.'
> 'Glory be!
> It can't be true!'

Train fades
Quickly,
In the distance, bound for London.
Legs stiff,
Walk starts,
Groans and breathless conversation.

'Got your butties?'
'Got your camera?'
'Is that a new anorak?'
'Wish I hadn't brought so much,
It's feeling heavy
On my back.'

Train's full.
Full of what?
Maps and muck and weary walkers.
Train takes
Back home
Nodding heads and tiring talkers.

'Where've you been, then,
Over Kinder?
Was it windy on the top?
Are you going for a noggin'
At the Bull's Head when we stop?'

Trekking back again a further generation from that lively account, it is an oddity – and also a reminder of how politicized a decade the '30s turned out to be – that while cycling through the Clarion Cycling Club and walking became closely identified with socialism, their popularity also owed something to the well publicized Strength Through Health cult in Germany; in other words, to the Nazis. On the right, Oswald Mosley flirted with Blackshirt camping rallies on the South Coast, and it is perhaps surprising that he did not pursue the idea as a means of welding his mainly working-class followers together. It would have seemed natural, after all, for a private army to muster in the age-old way that armies do, especially if it involved an activity known to be popular among many of its members; that having been said, Mosley was a man of patrician tastes, and in the end perhaps he simply had no stomach for weekends under canvas with the lads. Perhaps camping coaches, another child of the '30s, might have suited him slightly better. This was the railway companies' bright wheeze to latch on to a craze, and put old rolling stock into good use at the same time by converting redundant corridor carriages into caravans and shunting them into sidings at seaside stations and other pleasant places. By the outbreak of war the big four companies had nearly 450 of them dotted around the country, and the idea lived on for several years after nationalization.

But pinpointing the influence of politics on national trends is a luxury for those with the benefit of hindsight rather than the people caught up in them at the time. When you read of young boys in Germany joining the Hitler Youth Movement in the 1930s thinking it was an alternative to the Scouts, you can only believe them. By the same token, 99 per cent of youngsters who set off hiking and biking and camping in the 1930s did it simply because it was an escape from home, it was fun – and it was cheap. 'The first holiday I had was when I was 19 in the early '30s,' says Harry Bradshaw of south-east Lancashire. 'Four of us took a tent to Squires Gate, Blackpool, and they charged us 30s. a week, 7s. 6d. each. On top of that we knew a chap with a car who took us there and back with all our kit, so that wasn't bad, was it?' Cunningham's camp at Douglas on the Isle of Man, recalled elsewhere, was one of a number of major low-cost magnets, while for the tens of thousands of young people on the move there was an exciting new wave of Youth Hostels and cheap bed and breakfast stops approved by the Cyclists' Touring Club. The latter had its roots in an organization founded in 1878 and indeed has been operating under its present name since 1883. By the early years of the century it boasted a membership of some 60,000, and its large and distinctive enamel accommodation signs sprouted on cottage walls throughout the land; you will still see them, sometimes, though more often than not in collectors' and antiques markets with rather surprising sums of money written on labels on their backs.

Youth Hostels were yet another import from Germany, though they predated the rise of the Nazi health culture by some years, having been founded there before the First World War. They came comparatively late to this country, in 1930, the motivation stemming from the Liverpool area with a view to opening up North Wales to Merseyside youngsters, and Snowdonia was their first great stronghold. The original concept of Youth Hostels was for there to be strings of them in walking distance of each other, so that they could be reached by hikers in popular country areas without the need for any other kind of transport.

Indeed, cyclists were the only other travellers allowed to stay in them. It was certainly a cheap way to get around: in 1949, for instance, after people in the target age range of between 16 and 21 had paid their annual 5s. membership fee, their overnight charge was 2s. in summer and 1s. 6d. in winter; under-16s paid 1s. a year to join, with nightly fees ranging from 1s. in summer to 9d. in winter. At first the idea was for visitors to do their own cooking, bring their own sheet sleeping bag – 'flea-bags', as they instantly became known – to reduce laundry costs, and to perform some simple cleaning or maintenance task before moving on. But it was not long before wardens with suitable facilities realized that a cooked meal service would bring in a few coppers' extra revenue, and by 1949 you could have supper at many of England and Wales's 300 hostels for 1s. 9d. or 2s. The rise of the car-borne walker in the 1950s led to much bitter debate and agonizing in the YHA. Cars, after all, were by then scarcely the sole pre-serve of the affluent, yet there was still something about owning one and using one for the simple pursuit of enjoying the countryside that rankled among those who recalled the original ideals and aims of the movement.

Another way of tasting the fresh air was by taking a usually inappro-priately named pleasure flip in one of the great box-like biplanes that tootled round the skies of many of the big resorts in the inter-war years and into the 1950s. At Southport they landed on the beach, but Black-pool's aeroplane rides took off from the airport at Squires Gate, to the south of town. Melvyn Jones has particular cause to remember one of these in the early 1950s, when he and his parents took to the air for the first time ever, along with friends and neighbours out on a spree during Burnley wakes. 'I was the only child among the seven of us, and it had been a pretty miserable day for me,' he recalls. 'They had all been in Yates's Wine Lodge at dinner time, supping champagne at half a crown a glass or whatever it was, and after that they felt a cab down to Squires Gate and a flip round the Tower was the only possible way to finish off the afternoon. None of them had ever flown before, and I think they were all terrified. In fact they probably wouldn't have dreamed of doing it without that Yates's champers inside them. They were all a bit giggly on the tarmac, but it got really nightmarish when we climbed aboard. One of my dad's friends, Billy somebody, told them all a joke to relax them, one of Max Miller's. It was about a chap called Bert who was giv-ing a talk to his men's club about sex, except he told his wife it was about flying. The day after the meeting she was walking down the street when one of the club members stopped her and said:

'"That was a very good talk Bert gave us last night, Nellie."

'"That's funny," says Nellie. "He's only ever done it twice. The first time he was sick, and the second time his hat blew off."

'Well, because they were all nervous and giggly with champagne, they were all just falling around in the aeroplane at this, and I was seething because I didn't even get the joke. It got worse and worse, squeals as the plane bounced down the runway, shrieks when it took off; it was worst of all when it started circling the Tower, and this great thing just looked as if it was spinning round and round at an angle. It looked scary enough to me, but how it seemed to them in their tipsy state I can't imagine. It was certainly a weird introduction to flying. It's a wonder any of us ever set foot on an aircraft again.'

Those cheery crowds of couples, out on the sands with the kids during the day, or on the town for an hour or two at night after the youngsters had been tucked up; in the years after the two World Wars in particular, what gusto they put into simply enjoying each other's company, throwing themselves into daft games of beach ball with a blown-up football bladder more often than not patched up by an inner-tube repair kit, hooting with laughter if one of them should drop their ice cream wafer in the sand, and generally showing all the signs of school children let off the hook for the day. The war-time spirit was still with them – as indeed it needed to be, for there remained huge financial battles to be fought in both the early 1920s and the late '40s – but were they downhearted? No, even though in the austerity years following the 1939-45 conflict there were many who believed they had every right to be.

At the beginning of the wakes week of 1948 the *Rochdale Observer* suggested:

Our readers are entitled to expect something more than has been their lot in some of the post-war holidays in the way of travelling facilities, accommodation and opportunities to enjoy themselves in a reasonable way without being required to pay through the nose for those little pleasures which make up a pleasant and carefree holiday. We are glad to note that British Railways are meeting the tremendous wakes demand for an expanded service of through trains to the popular resorts. This is a much appreciated concession, and although there is nothing cheap about present-day railway fares – which are practically double those of ten years ago – the increased service of trains should offer a reasonable prospect of comfortable travel. The average Englishman on holiday is one of the most long-suffering individuals on earth; otherwise he would never have tolerated the fight to board overcrowded trains, the dirty carriages and the inconceivable lack of facilities for obtaining light refreshments, even on long-distance trains, which has too long been associated with holiday travel on the railways. This is a matter which should concern British Railways just as much as the move to give rolling stock the 'New Look' and brighten many of our gloomy and depressing stations. The fact that money is definitely tighter than was the case 12 months ago may not be a bad thing for the holidaymaker, for it should knock the bottom out of many scandalous 'rackets' – in accommodation, meals, ice cream and entertainment prices – which have flourished since the end of the war.

Grumbles about prices shooting up after the nationalization of the railways will doubtless be brought to a neat full circle some time in the 1990s, when there will be even louder grumbles about their shooting up even more after denationalization. And as for the spivs in their Arthur English-style zoot suits, one can only imagine that their fiendish plot to charge the innocent holiday-maker through the nose for his ice cream did not come to much, since penny wafers and cornets survived well into the 1950s. It is surprising to recall just how much resentment did spill over from the war years, and in what quirky ways. On holiday in the late 1940s we put up with all manner of irksomeness without complaint: food and clothing rationing, queuing and all the constraints of an almost touchingly austere lifestyle, when it is viewed in hindsight. Yet there seemed no real impetus to plunge headlong into new ways, little zest for the old order changing after that remarkable rush to the head, very un-English, of the 1945 general election. Brian Whittle, brought up near Cleckheaton, remembers the seething anger of his father and uncles when imported American fads like hot dogs and Coca-Cola first started appearing in the seafront stalls and kiosks of Bridlington in the early '50s. 'It wasn't a question of my dad and his brothers not liking Coke and hot dogs,' he says. 'In fact I doubt whether they had ever tasted them. What it was was far deeper than that, closely bound up with the British serviceman's "overpaid, over-sexed and over here" view of the GIs in this country during the war. They vilified those snacks as if they were poison, singing the praises of good old Yorkshire fish and chips and making this foreign stuff sound unimaginably decadent, evil – and, of course, glamorous. I think one of the biggest let-downs of my life was years later, when I was about 14 and out of their clutches for the day, parting with 1s. 6d. for a hot dog in a steamy little café near some railway arches in Accrington. What was the fuss all about . . .?'

# CHAPTER 8

# *Huddersfield's Baker From Mars*

'Wakes week was a dreary time to me when I was a little girl,' says Sally Robertson, looking back to her childhood in Church, near Accrington, in the years immediately after the First World War. 'My father was chief engineer at Steiner's mill, where they made Turkey Red dye, and while everyone else was away he had to stay at home to be there while the boilers were inspected. All I knew was that there was nobody to play with, the place was deadly silent with all the factory whistles and hooters hushed, and the shops that weren't shut were going at half pace. I suppose, looking back, there were more folks around than there might have been, since this was the Depression, and there were lots who couldn't afford to go away. But Church, Accrington and Oswaldtwistle, which shared the same week, really were ghost towns for those few days. Some people went on day trips in the Ribble Valley, to Whalley or Clitheroe, and if money was really tight you could always walk up the Coppice, the hill overlooking Accrington, and marvel at the sight of the town without the factory chimneys belching. But we had no wakes fair, like lots of the big towns, and I don't blame the showmen. They wouldn't have had much to show by the end of their week in Accrington.' Writing about a visit to north-east Lancashire more than a generation later, Mike Harding, the noted comedian, folklorist and Northern social historian, caught the spirit of the occasion, if not perhaps quite the literal truth, when he wrote: 'I remember once cycling through Burnley during their wakes week. I sat on the saddle of my bike in the town centre for almost an hour, and the only moving things I saw were a dog and the hands of the Town Hall clock.'

Mike Harding and Sally Robertson do not paint too enticing a picture

Likeness-takkin' shop: you did not have to be beside the seaside to make believe you were.

of wakes week life for the stay-at-homes, and Mary Carter of Huddersfield's account is scarcely more alluring. 'My dad worked out of town
when I was growing up in the '30s, so we were not tied to the Huddersfield holidays,' she recalls. 'I worked in a baker's shop in my early
teens, just a little two-man business, and during the wakes my poor old
boss never knew what to do, whether to stay open all day, go part-time
or simply abandon his customers who had stayed at home and make off
with the trippers. Whatever it was, he was always wrong. I was with
him for three years, and I remember he never knew from day to day
whether he'd not sell a loaf or be cleaned out of stock by 11 in the morning. "I don't know, Mary," he'd say. "Fifty-one weeks a year I know
what folk round here want to the last teacake, but on weeks like this I
might as well be a man from Mars for all I know about Huddersfield."
There was one day when we'd sat around all afternoon, from dinner
time, without a soul coming in the shop, until at about half past four he
said: "That's it, lass, let's call it a day." The next morning we'd not been
open ten minutes before women were streaming in playing hell because
they'd come at ten to five and hadn't been able to get bread for the kids'
tea. That just about summed up wakes week as far as my boss and I
were concerned.'

David Webb of Bolton also remembers stay-at-home holidays in the
1930s as a time of strife. 'My dad worked Manchester way, nothing to
do with cotton, so the wakes didn't mean much to us,' he recalls. 'The
only way the mills had any impact on our lives was with their hooters
– we used them as time checks throughout the day, and of course you
could set your clocks by them when you could recognize their individual tones. The first time check was the early morning call – so no
working day, no hooter, no alarm clock. The result was that my dad
would oversleep, miss the bus, and arrive up to an hour late at this
quite high-powered city firm of his where life regulated by the mill
whistle all seemed light years away. The first time it happened his
boss took it in good spirit. He and most of my dad's colleagues lived
on the Cheshire side, and even in the '30s they tended to think he was
a bit old-fashioned living in Bolton – jokes about George Formby and
Our Gracie and all that. But when his late arrival went on day after
day it all got a bit serious, and one night he came home really believ-
ing he'd get the sack if it happened again. I was about ten at the time,
and it worried me terribly. I remember my mother ended up borrow-
ing two or three alarm clocks from neighbours who were also staying
at home but on holiday from work, so in no need of an early call.

They did the trick – but I didn't really sleep easily until the hooters were going again.'

Harry Bradshaw, who grew up in south-east Lancashire during the Depression, puts at as low as 25 per cent the number of people who were able to afford to go away at that time, and indeed through much of the '30s. For him, at least, the image of whole towns utterly deserted is an erroneous one, though he admits that over and above that 25 per cent there would be others off on day trips and yet more happy enough to lie low at home and recharge their batteries for another year; combined with the mill and shop closures, a visiting stranger might well have concluded that everyone had up and left. 'In the days before paid holidays, there was no way a man with three or four young children could have afforded to go away,' he swears. 'That unpaid week was a real blow to a lot of people, and there would never be any shortage of workers volunteering to go in and whitewash the factory while it was quiet. The engineers and maintenance men would do the technical jobs in the shutdown, but anyone could volunteer for Buxton flatting, as they called the whitewashing. It was a Godsend to lots of people who found it hard to manage.'

More positive memories come from Ted McGrath, who grew up in Blackburn in the 1950s. 'I had five brothers and sisters, so there wasn't much cash around our house,' he recalls. 'It meant we never went away to stay, which upset my mum but didn't bother us at all.

'"We've decided to go on days this year," she'd tell the neighbours every year, as if she and my dad had sat down in the front room with a pile of brochures from Florida and the Bahamas, pored through them for hours and then tossed them aside saying: "Nah, let's stop in Blackburn and go on days instead." But the thing was, we had a marvellous time on those day trips on the train or coach. When we were very little kids we never knew in advance where we were going on any given day, so it might be Blackpool or it might be Belle Vue Zoo in Manchester or it might be up on the moors above Darwen with sausages and eggs fried on an open fire at the end of it. At the beginning of the week we'd wake up in the morning thinking: "I wonder where it will be today." And the point was, wherever it was it was magical, and by the middle and end of the week we felt we'd done and seen so much that a day at home drawing or playing a lazy game of soccer in the street seemed magical, too, as well as not doing our dad's wallet any harm. I honestly felt no envy at all for my pals away in Blackpool or Morecambe. As far as I was concerned, Blackburn with no school for me and no work for my mum and dad was so far removed from real life that it might as well have been Rio.'

But the shop closures were depressing for less cheerfully inclined stay-at-homes, and there was little comfort to be had from the lists in the local newspapers of the post offices and chemists who would conde-scend to open for an hour or two now and then, or the points where newspapers might be collected in the absence of any kind of delivery service. 'It was easier to buy a copy of the *Evening Telegraph* in Blackpool than it was in Blackburn in wakes week,' Margaret Jennings of Fenis-cowles recalls. 'You'd go to the big West Coast resorts in the Blackburn holidays and you'd see the local paper everywhere.' The Yorkshire and Lancashire evening papers would set great store by this gesture, to the extent of packing off a couple of reporters and photographers for the week to record their fellow townsfolk at play. As a bonus there would always be stories to be written about some little lad hurt climbing a cliff or a big lad hurt colliding with an even bigger lad's fist after closing time, and if a home-town family found itself marooned on a rock and the lifeboat was turned out, that was joy indeed. Even the smaller weekly papers got in on the act – and a worthwhile public relations exercise they found it, for the sake of giving a vanman an afternoon out by the sea. The *Rochdale Observer*, for example, could be bought at eight shops in Blackpool, St Anne's, Poulton-le-Fylde and Southport during the town's main holiday in the 1930s. But if you wanted to buy a loaf of bread back home? That could be a different matter, as Alan and Doris Smith of Whitefield, near Manchester, recall. 'It would have been possible to starve in some towns in wakes week,' they say. 'It was no joke for old people left behind if they didn't have neighbours keeping an eye on them.'

For towns such as Rochdale, without wakes funfairs, those of gloomy disposition could certainly be made to feel they had been left high and dry. At the beginning of the August rushbearing holiday of 1923, the *Rochdale Observer* published a column of ten 'Holiday Jaunts Near Home – Some Fine Walks Accessible From Rochdale.' Those seeking inspira-tion probably threw the paper aside in disappointment as the usual litany of Norden, Ashworth Valley, Heaton Park and the dreaded Boggart Hole Clough in the North Manchester suburbs was trotted out for yet another year. My memory of Boggart Hole Clough in the 1950s was as a place one would be threatened with as a punishment, 'If you're good we'll go up on Holcombe Hill this Sunday; if you're bad we'll go to Boggart Hole Clough', and I can scarcely imagine it was much more exciting in 1923. The *Observer's* more inspired suggestions that year included Haworth, which involved taking a train to Keighley and walking the eleven miles to the station at Hebden Bridge, taking in the Brontë village *en route*; another walk, this one of thirteen miles, taking the train to Colne and hiking again to Hebden Bridge, this time via Widdop reservoir and Heptonstall; and Hollingworth Lake, the 'aquatic and other' attractions of which the newspaper ventured to suggest its readers had not forgotten. 'These are only a few of the many ways by which, making judicious use of tram or train, the holidaymaker may gain easy access to pleasant cloughs and woods, and the invigorating moorlands of which too few know the charm and the benefit,' the *Observer* concluded.

But the paper was right in supposing that Hollingworth Lake was high on every stay-at-home's list of day trips. Created in the years around 1800 as a reservoir for the Rochdale Canal, it had been a magnet since 1839, when the railway came to Littleborough, and by the 1850s and '60s it was blessed by such attractions as paddle steamers, boats for hire, a regatta and two grand hotels in the Lake and the Beach, the first of which was soon offering such joys as ready access to the pleasure grounds, quoits and a skating rink with Plumpton's Patent Roller Skates. Little was ever mentioned in print of the lake's almost surrealistically cold water, but no matter; if Blackpool was the 'Weighvers' Paradise' then this was surely the 'Weighvers' Seaport', and a guide of the 1860s left you in no doubt that as tripper resorts went, it was the real thing:

> You are out of your everyday world – transported suddenly from regions of smoke and dust and the sound of busy life to where Nature herself appears to be making holiday. You will see Blackstone Edge to the east, towering above its fellows, and preaching from its rocky pulpit sermons to the solitude around; the lone White House nestling in the dip of the moor, and the grey band of road winding up to the breast, until it is lost on the summit. If it be an holiday, and the weather fine, woe to you if you come to enjoy an hour's solitude, for the lake is teeming with life. Shooting towards every point, as if they were engaged in performing an aquatic reel, an apparently countless number of boats are plying. Oars are flashing in the sun, and white sails are fluttering and gliding about as if they took as natural to fresh water as salt. The ferry steamer is churning its direct course backwards and forwards betwixt the landing stage and the pleasure gar-

dens on the other side of the water. With very brief intervals you see it dividing the array of smaller craft, which sheer out of its way from wholesome fear of being stove in or caught in its swell. For the fee of a penny you may take a passage on board and make acquaintance with what we once heard facetiously termed 'Th' Cheshire Side'. Probably you are like other excursionists, who immediately they leave home fancy themselves in need of refreshments; so if you feel concerned about the 'inner man', you may get a cup of coffee or tea and a 'real Eccles cake' at one of the numerous places which crowd the vicinity of the landing stage.

A fairground was a vital ingredient in the early days, and fairs have been coming and going to and from Hollingworth Lake ever since, the hot food and drink sellers doing as well as ever as dusk descends and the inevitable chill comes in off the water. A big attraction in the inter-war years, and indeed into the late '40s, was a grand old 'Bobby Horse' roundabout, steam-powered in its early days, which was well into its eighties when it took up a new lease of life in New Brighton. Even after that, the splendid six-feet-high horses went out glamorously to grass in

The wakes fair at Oldham's Tommyfield shortly before the First World War.

the United States, where it is hard to believe that they are not some ardent collector's pride and joy. But for visitors to wakes weeks fairs all over the North in the golden years those great prancing horses, their manes streaming and their golden harnesses aglint, were just part of a magical world of light and music and noise. The recent revival of interest in vintage fairground organs and rides powered by steam-generated electricity give us some pale insight into a night out at a wakes fair seventy or so years ago, but our modern-day vision can only begin to appreciate the impact on dark, inward-looking and careworn communities of these great gaudy, hissing, screaming monsters that would descend on the market places and spread through the very streets themselves for this once-a-year week. Danger was never far below the surface – the hard, mean boxers at the booths, looking almost like a different species of creature from the cocky youths they hoped might challenge them; the naked naphtha flares at dusk, a constant threat to the canvas stalls; silly rides like the cake walk for the local hobbledehoys, jiggling them around on swinging platforms as they struggled to keep their last four pints down; rifle ranges where stray ricochets always seemed set to put your eye out; and the constantly lurking uncertainty about the safety of ancient timber rides forever on the move across the length and breadth of the North of England, losing a nut here, a bolt there, fraying a rope at Barnsley, sheering a chain at Nelson.

They were quite the place for gourmets, of course, with their hot potatoes, brandy snaps, coconuts, ice cream and even the fresh fruits of the season, such as plums. In her book of Stalybridge recollections, *Down Memory Lane*, Joyce Shaw remembers Butterworth's black pea saloon down by the river, and the locals joking that that was where they had been soaked overnight to give them that extra tang. Mrs Shaw has another memory of the wakes fair, too, one that reminds us just how much the old-style fairground was the creation of a world far removed from our own: 'About Thursday morning the first wagons would arrive, watched by many children after a free ride when the roundabouts were erected and slowly tried out before the crowds started to roll up. About this time the inmates of the Ashton Workhouse could be seen in their rough grey clothing. They were walked down and given free rides whilst it was quiet, and there would be gifts of fruit and sweets to take back with them.'

By the 1930s the big, traditional wakes funfairs were the exception rather than the rule, and as Sally Robertson remarked, it was hardly surprising; although they were hugely welcomed by those who were around home, and the sight of them in the usually busy streets was graphic proof that the town was at play, you could hardly blame the showmen for thinking twice about setting up for a week in a Marie Celeste of a town in which a final dry Saturday evening, with the rovers returning by their tens of thousands, was the only night of certain success. There were all kinds of small attractions quite forgotten now – a 1948 *Rochdale Observer* advertisement for the Riviera open-air pool at Norden, with its sandpit, paddling pool, tea terrace and pleasant café is a timely reminder that on the right kind of day a couple with young children could while away many happy hours at little expense – but by and large, the 'ghost town' tag seemed apt enough for the stay-at-homes.

During the Second World War, of course, with the coast barred to trippers, a few days off at home was the best that could be expected, short of a brief visit to some pleasant country spot. Local authorities recognized this and organized Holidays At Home programmes, some-

A war-time Holidays At Home canal cruise from Leigh Bridge in Lancashire, organized by the local cable works in 1942.

times quite imaginative projects that cast the grey men in embattled Northern town halls as impresarios for the week. There was a fuss in Rochdale in 1942 when the entertainments lost £1,200, having cost some £3,200 and brought in ticket sales of just £2,000, but the list of some forty offerings speaks of a genuine attempt to entertain all with bands, concert parties, a celebrity concert, dances, a dog and pet show, donkey rides, marionettes, a swimming gala, a vegetable and flower show, paddle boats, Punch and Judy and a roundabout in Springfield Park. The big loss-makers were the bands and food vans, the latter failure perhaps telling us all we need to know about war-time catering, but the picture was made blacker by the fact that all the costs had been totted up in the final reckoning, including the council staff's time and resources. Rochdale Town Hall hit back at critics who felt this was a poor result by arguing that other towns that had apparently balanced their books better during Holidays At Home week had massaged their figures by 'losing' the bills for corporation services in other budgets. It had been felt best to let the enterprise 'stand on its own feet', the council declared, in a phrase strangely prophetic of the spirit of local government fifty years later.

In times of war and peace, Belle Vue Zoo and Pleasure Grounds near Manchester were a great draw for the mill towns around the fringes of the city, but they could never be seen as a cheap alternative to a day out in Southport or Blackpool, as Tom Anderson of Mytholmroyd recalls: 'You might have saved a few shillings on the fare, but once there you were in an old-style showman's paradise of funfairs, speedway, freak shows, candy floss and death-defying stuntmen on motorbikes that could make Blackpool's Golden Mile look like Bond Street. You soon felt that it was only the animals in their cramped cages who hadn't lost their human dignity and weren't after your money, but it was depressing to stay with them for too long. I can't say that at the age of four in 1950 I was an animal rights campaigner in a way that would have much credence today, and I enjoyed lumbering round on the howdah on the elephant's back as much as anybody. But I do know that even at that age, I was completely baffled by Belle Vue's policy of putting on big, noisy Saturday night firework pageants with all those animals caged just a little way away. We all knew from Bonfire Night that fireworks and animals didn't mix, but there we were watching the Relief of Mafeking in sky rockets and bangers.

'There were freak shows there, too, almost to the bitter end of Belle Vue's days as a zoo and funfair. Even in the mid-1970s I remember seeing an Irishman there who was buried alive for so many days to create a world record. He was in a decent-sized glass-topped cell down a hole, with a pipe up for food and air, and it looked a comfortable enough existence. It reminded me very much of those stunts on Blackpool Prom in the '30s, but this was forty years on from then. Years before that at Belle Vue I remember a show purporting to be an Amazonian jungle woman, growing on a vine. I paid my couple of bob and walked along past a brightly-lit tableau of green leaves, and in the midst of it all was a woman with a green-painted face whose head seemed to be growing out of the top of a drainpipe, painted in a similar green. I admit it was clever; I couldn't see how it was done, and she was a real woman all right. So there I was in this booth, the only one in the place, and face-to-face with her, just a few feet apart. I didn't know what to do or say. In the end I said "How do" or something original like that, and she answered in kind. She sounded to come from the Wigan end of the Amazon jungle. On another occasion I saw quite a decent show, in which a chap invited members of the audience to step into his cabinet and disappear before our very eyes. A brave girl went up into an open-fronted sentry box with three mirrors as its inside walls, the showman then turned on some intensely bright lights and sure enough, you watched her fade away until there was nothing. I must say it was a clever effect; it was certainly the first and only time I saw a person disappear in thin air, other than in trick photography.

'On the other side of the coin, I think the most pathetic sideshow I ever saw was also at Belle Vue. It was a dwarf with an accordion who billed himself the human juke-box. He was sitting there with a handwritten list of 100 tunes beside him, and if you shouted fifty-eight he'd strike up with *Singing The Blues*, or whatever. It was clever, I suppose; I can scarcely think of a more profitable way of putting an accordion-playing dwarf who knew 100 tunes to good use. The last time I was at Belle Vue I was with a friend of mine from Preston, Norman Wiggins, and we were walking past the spot where the human juke-box had been. I was just telling him about it, and we were laughing, when a little sparrow came thundering through the air straight at his head, and poor old Norman had to duck sharpish to miss it. That was something else I'd never seen before. There was always something odd in the air at Belle Vue. It was never to me the happy and carefree place it was cracked up to be. The best thing about it was the trolley buses that took you there from the middle of Manchester in the late '40s. It was the only time I rode on trolley buses, and their strange whine and the sparks flying from the wires made them as deliciously scary to me as almost any ride on the funfair apart from the Bobs, that huge and ancient timber big dipper they had at Belle Vue. They talk about white knuckle rides at Alton Towers and Blackpool Pleasure Beach today – but it adds an extra dimension of terror to a ride when you're not absolutely certain that the whole damned thing isn't going to collapse under you, and that was certainly the way I felt about the Bobs in its later days.'

In the inter-war years Saturday night dancing trips to the Tower or Winter Gardens at Blackpool were big sellers, the all-in price of around 2s. working out at 1s. 6d. or so for the fare and 6d. for admission to the dancehall. They were a top draw right through the season, but the wakes specials were different again for the stay-at-homes. 'It was best to go on the last Saturday of the holidays,' says Peter Artingstall, who grew up in Bolton in the 1920s. 'On the first Saturday, with so many people off to Blackpool for the week, it was a bit miserable thinking you'd be on the train back home in a few hours' time. But if you left it till the last Saturday, when everybody else was coming home, it made you feel good to be off to the seaside as they were all trailing off the trains looking cheesed off to be home on the opposite platform. It was nice on the Sunday night, too, on the weekly monkey run when all the boys and girls met up together and flirted and gossiped. The Sunday night at the end of the wakes was always lively, with people getting together again and so much new to report to each other, and if you'd been on the dancing trip the previous evening it was good to be able to say "When I were in t'Tower last neet . . .", and really mean it.'

# CHAPTER 9

# *Happiest Days Of The Year*

And how did they come about, our wakes holidays? It must readily be confessed that that term was not in universal use through our towns, but whatever we called them, we took them so much for granted as children – only to learn in later life that like so many other working people's blessings, they were shaped by a combination of tradition, occasional flashes of enlightenment, and far more often by our fore-fathers' sheer dogged bloody-mindedness. What is certain is that in the beginning were the holy days, the festivals that honoured the patron saint of the local parish church. These would keep the priest and his faithful congregation literally 'a-wake' praying and keeping vigil from the eve of the big day through until dawn – but come morning, far greater numbers of parishioners would be out in the streets, squares and greens to help them celebrate in more lively ways – and as early as 800 years ago, the holiday element of the holy days was beginning to show through, with drinking and games, and hawkers selling food, ribbons and trinkets. As a break from the mean routine of life and a chance to reunite with friends and relatives from the surrounding countryside, these fairs grew ever more important to people through the Middle Ages – the happiest days of the year, in fact, in the long centuries of his-tory before Christmas or birthdays began to mean very much in our forefathers' lives.

The reason our Northern wakes tradition grew away from these holi-day fair days in a different way from the rest of Britain is fairly obvious. Lancashire and the West Riding were at the heart of the beginnings of the Industrial Revolution 200 years ago, and it became clear to the factory managers from the start that to operate efficiently they had to organize their employees' hours of work – and thus their hours of rest – to a degree that would have been irrelevant and impossible in the many communities nationwide where the pattern of life was still much as it had been in Tudor and Stuart times. But long before the Industrial Revolution – right back, indeed, to Tudor times and the reign of Henry VIII – the first stirrings of organized labour were already making their mark on the wakes, and taking them away from festivals observed strictly on the day of individual town and villages' patron saint. Merrie England had long since accepted holy days as fun holidays for workers – and since agreements such as guild apprenticeships and indentures were not restricted by parish boundaries, by the early sixteenth century they had so many high days and holidays written into them that there was genuine concern that they would affect the trading performance of the nation. Puritans of Bluff King Hal's day were particularly concerned that as well as curtailing work, the wakes were sliding into a tradition of drunkenness and rowdyism, much of it in and around the church; the result, in any event, was an Act of 1536 that decreed that the feast of the dedication of every church should be celebrated on the same day, the first Sunday in October. This was all still a very long way from the communal wakes holiday we know, but it set the precedent for switching the celebrations from inconvenient dates to more acceptable ones. Centuries later in Victorian times it was echoed in the textile towns of Lancashire and Yorkshire when communities with patronal festivals in the grey months of the year switched their holidays to more promising high summer dates.

Less than fifty years after Henry VIII's Act, in 1579, Elizabeth I felt the need to institute a commission to reform the manners of her subjects. West of the Pennines, for instance, the Bishop of Chester and his advisers met in Manchester to issue orders forbidding 'pipers and minstrels playing, making and frequenting bear-baiting and bull-baiting on the Sabbath days, or upon any other days in time of divine service; and also against superstitious ringing of bells, wakes and common feasts . . . .'. A very different message came through when James I was passing through Lancashire from Scotland in 1617, as a guest of Sir Richard de Hoghton. By this time, with Puritanism the rallying point of Parliamentary opposition to the king, the pursuit or otherwise of pleasure was at the heart of the political agenda. James lost no time in making it plain to the county's strait-laced governors that his subjects there should not be denied

# Sea Bathing.

The Public are respectfully informed that an OMNIBUS called

# THE SAFETY

Will commence Running to the SIMPSON'S HOTEL,

# BLACKPOOL,

## On Wednesday, the 21st May, 1845,

## From the HOLE IN THE WALL INN, in COLNE,

### And from the OLD RED LION INN, BURNLEY,

*Through Blackburn, Preston, and Lytham to Blackpool Three Times a Week, viz.—*

On Wednesdays and Fridays from Colne, starting at Six o'clock in the Morning, and leaving Burnley at Seven o'clock, and reaching Blackpool at Two o'clock in the Afternoon, and on Monday Mornings from Burn'ey at Seven o'clock.

The above Omnibus will leave Blackpool returning to the above places every Tuesday, Thursday, and Saturday, at Ten o'clock in the Forenoon.

*N. B. Arrangements will be made so that Passengers will be able to proceed through to Blackpool, without stopping except for change of Horses.*

PERFORMED BY THE PUBLICS MOST OBEDIENT SERVANTS

## STUTTARD, ALLEN, & Co.

H. EARNSHAW, PRINTER COLNE

A coach for sea bathers to Blackpool three times a week from Colne in May 1945, reminding us that trips to the coast were popular in Lancashire before the railway era. The journey took eight hours, from 6 a.m. until 2 p.m., with the return leaving Blackpool at 10 a.m. the following day – but with the arrival of the railway at the resort in the same year, time was fast running out for the stagecoach.

their lawful recreations so long as the Sabbath was not desecrated, and he stressed their rights to the 'having of May-games, Whitson-ales and Morice-dances, and the setting up of Maypoles . . .'. Come the revolution, of course, and the rise to power of the Puritans in the Civil War, such cheerful instructions counted for nothing. And come the counter-revolution? Not surprisingly, the backlash was swift and joyous, with England again throwing itself into fairs and wakes and festivals as if its life and soul depended on them.

And that was the way it stayed through the eighteenth century into the Industrial Revolution, when it soon became evident to the first generation of mass employers that the charms of the loom and the weaving shed could not bear a candle to a good old beano that had been part of the local scene for generations. Absenteeism and unreliability of workers was one of the first crosses the early mill owners had to bear; there was, after all, no tradition of regimented labour on this scale, and the concept of being a member of a disciplined work-force simply did not come into the reckoning. Bull-baiting was a big draw in the Manchester area until well into the 1830s, and travelling charlatans with an eye for

When rushbearing was a rough old trade: a rush cart in the Manchester area in 1821.

the main chance could still catch the public's imagination in quite spectacular fashion. There was a famous day in 1854, for instance, when one
Monseigneur Signor de la Unsinque declared that he would walk web-
footed on water at Padiham fair in a chariot drawn by geese; the prospect all but brought Burnley to a standstill, and the crowds flocked in
over the tops from as far afield as Bacup to the south, Barrowford and
Colne to the north-east. It is a reminder that in spite of the thumb-nail
rule that human nature never changes, people in general were so much
different then, so removed from our bland and understated twentieth
century that one might almost be talking about another species. Lovers
of Dickens will know how his characters laugh and cry and throw their
arms about each other and flare in rage in ways quite alien to our British
culture – though perhaps such conduct does not seem so foreign to present-day Americans, Italians or Israelis. Dickens was not exaggerating in
these accounts of his fellow man, and older readers can doubtless look
back on their childhood and think of numerous 'characters' of whom it
can be said with literal truth that 'they don't make 'em like that any
more'. In short, the first wave of mill workers did not consist of fore-
lock-tugging serfs cowed into doing their masters' bidding. They were a
spiky, awkward bunch of lads and lasses – and if they said it was holiday time, then holiday time it was.

In south-east Lancashire, particularly in Rochdale and Oldham and
smaller towns around them, the wakes were linked closely with the
ancient ceremony of rushbearing; indeed, the holidays are still 'rushber-
rin' to older folks in Rochdale, though that usage seems certain to die
out within a generation, in spite of successful efforts to revive the actual
ceremony there. The custom of strewing fresh rushes on the stone floors
of churches at around harvest time was common in the fifteenth and sixteenth centuries, and as early as 1642 there was an entry in the church-
wardens' accounts at Rochdale parish church recording that 5s. was
paid for 'getting out rushes and sweeping out the church'. Five years
later the sexton received 1s. for ringing on rushbearing day. As with
every annual church festival, a ceremony grew up around this simple
practice, with parishioners going out on to the moorland where the
rushes grew on the Saturday, and bearing them back to the church with
decorations of flowers and garlands. On the Sunday, with the church
floor newly strewn and the flowers decorating its walls, the parson
could always rely on a full congregation; and on the Monday everyone
took the day off work as the flowers were carried through the town.
Problems began with the introduction of floorboards and the end of a

practical need for what was, after all, the strictly secular aim of making the church more comfortable for worshippers in winter. The task of cutting the rushes, not unnaturally, had gone to the big, tough lads of the community – and this being an exhausting job on a hot August afternoon, drink had crept into the formula quite early in the ceremony's history. At the beginning of the Industrial Revolution, in 1780, the vicar of Rochdale reflected widespread unease about the abuse of the occasion when he found it necessary to forbid rushes being brought into church on the Saturday night, and for the next few decades rushbearing took a very different turn.

It was then that the rushcart made its appearance, bearing a huge pyramid of rushes, still decorated with garlands and ribbons. Some thirty or forty young men in white shirts and sashes – in other words, typical morris dancers' garb – would be harnessed to it in pairs, dragging it round town from pub to pub accompanied by a band, jingling copper bells and stamping time to the music with their wooden clogs. A clown dressed as a sluttish woman, 'Dirty Molly' or 'Dirty Bet', would collect money for their refreshment, and after the pubs had been exhausted they would continue to the homes of the local gentry, where the ladies of the house would customarily give them more cash and garlands from the garden. There would be further dancing on a piece of ground first swept by 'Dirty Molly', and the nobs would be invited to admire the banner into which the lads' wives, mothers and girlfriends had invested many hours' work. A matter of great pride and rivalry were the banners, with neighbouring villages vying with each other for the most eye-catching; in the Rochdale area honours often went to Marland, and if something or someone was 'as bonny as a Marland banner' it was high praise indeed.

Away from the grounds of the gentry's villas, life on the rushcarts was not quite so genteel. In the big towns there would be perhaps a dozen carts parading on the big day, and when they met each other the encounter would end either in fisticuffs or, if the teams and their bodyguards happened to be friendly, much jeering and waving of favours and going off for yet another noggin. Pubs were the focal point of most of the teams in later days, and their regulars and their families rallied round with great enthusiasm in the weeks leading up to the event. Perhaps the closest equivalent in England today is the carnival tradition in Somerset, where largely pub- and club-based teams in mainly working-class towns such as Bridgwater, Highbridge and Yeovil go to extraordinary lengths to produce illuminated floats which gather together at various set venues during a short season of usually damp November evenings, competing against one another, drawing crowds that put the FA Cup Final to shame and at the same time raising many thousands of pounds for charity. As for the Lancashire rushbearers, there was even more beer money at the end of it all, since the banners would invariably go to the pawn shops and the rushes, no longer required by the vicar, would be knocked down to the highest bidder.

Another rough-and-ready piece of folklore that has come down through the years is a wakes song that apparently originated in Wood-houses and had found its way to Droylsden by 1814. It is a knockabout comedy act between a supposed husband and wife, arguing between themselves bitterly as they worked furiously to see who could spin flax the faster on an old-fashioned wheel. There are often suggestive sexual undertones in songs like this, referring to prowess at spinning or weaving or other physical pursuits, but that is not apparent here. What is clear is that they liked their comedy broad and rough at the old wakes celebrations, as this couple of verses demonstrates. To add flavour, the folk song collector Brian Hollingsworth suggests that in Droyslden at least, the whole rigmarole took place on horseback, with the 'wife' being a man in drag and both parties collecting money from the crowds at the same time:

Woman: Theaw brags o' thisel', bur Aw dunno think it's true,
For Aw will uphowd thi' fawts aren't a few;
For when theau has done, un spun very hard
O' this Aw'm well sure, thi work is ill marred.

Man: Theaw saucy old jade, theaw'd best hold thi tung,
Or else Aw's be thumpin' thi ere it be lung,
Un iv ot Aw do, theaw'rt sure for to rue,
For Aw con ha' monny o' one as good as you.

The song is sometimes known as Threedywheel because of its chorus:

So it's threedywheel, threedywheel
Dan, don, dill, doe.

Music that fell somewhat short of society entertainment was only the half of it. In the 1830s rushbearing in Oldham, Uppermill and Saddle-worth was a riot of bull-baiting and other dubious jollities; but Victorian respectability, the rising cost of putting on a show because of the drainage of rush-growing marshes close to the towns  – and not least, the chance to get away on a cheap excursion to the sea – took swift toll after that, and by 1848 the Ashton-under-Lyne journalist Richard Oastler felt the need to use his radical newspaper, *The Champion,* to put in the strongest defence of a custom that had acquired potent political undertones in its symbolism of the common man's free spirit in the face of establishment oppression:

> If the church need no rushes, lads and lassies need a holiday. And how are they to have it, if there be no dread authority to curb the greedy masters who would take it from them? . . . Do monster mills answer better for the workman than his old loom house on the farmstead, his mother's wheel and spindle in the nook? Are prowling policemen and teetotal gawbies better moralists at a rushbearing than swings, whirligigs and show booths, stalls, toys and spice, jack-pudding, merriman and that prince of popular instructors, 'old father Punch'? . . . Hurrah for Oldham wakes! And till rich men give us better wage and wise men find us better pastime, may no foreign cutthroats put down the harmless mirth of morris dance and rushbearing . . . . Why wish to put it down? Where is the awful sin of keeping up these pastimes of olden time? For the life of us we cannot find it out. It seems as if some men are doing all they could to make the people hate them. Do, do give over with you, and let folks be!

But contrast this with August 1871, when the *Rochdale Observer* could report of Milnrow wakes:

> This annual festival has once more been celebrated under the happiest auspices so far as the weather is concerned. On Sunday there was a large influx of visitors to the village, and on Monday the carnival was at its height. Besides the attractions which have come to be inseparably associated with the wakes, such as pea saloons, toy stalls and hobby horses, a feature has been introduced which has been absent from the festival of late years, though formerly it was one of the most prominent. We refer to the rushcart, which on Monday was dragged through the streets at the tail of a lot of boys, divested, however, of what in former times constituted one of the chief glories of the affair, the gay decorations of ribbons etc. Tuesday was a very quiet day, the village being comparatively deserted, nearly 1,000 of the inhabitants

having taken advantage of the facilities afforded them to breathe for a few hours the pure sea air. The church schools went to Llandudno, the trip consisting of about 300 persons, and the Sunday School Union trip this year was to the 'Queen of Watering Places', Scarborough. Nearly 600 availed themselves of this latter excursion. Both trains arrived home about midnight, the journeys having been satisfactorily accomplished.

By the early 1870s, then, the rushcart had been reduced, in this mill village at least, to a folksy revival for the entertainment of the children. Such a state of affairs pleased the temperance-supporting *Rochdale Observer*, though the liberal *Oldham Chronicle* followed Richard Oastler's line by being staunch in its defence of the revellers until deep into the century. There had been riots over an election victory by the Liberals in Oldham in 1847, the year before Oastler's diatribe, and more trouble at the rushbearing a few weeks later; and in 1861, with rumours of fights between locals and Irish navvies rife, magistrates saw the chance they had long awaited and passed by-laws banning the carts. There was no shortage of those who turned out in defiance, but the day passed quietly enough – not least because of the efforts of one staunch constable who, fearing a battle, stood at a toll gate and 'threatened to break the skull of any man amongst them who passed through'. The ban prompted the *Chronicle* to pronounce: 'If rush carts are obstructive, so are Whit processions. Whether they are immoral is irrelevant. The bench has no business with morals, and will not be allowed to ride roughshod over the people's pastimes and their ancient customs without protest, so long as there is a free press in the country and a free spirit in its people.'

Such sentiments were swimming against the tide, however, and less than ten years later, in 1870, the *Chronicle* was reporting that there had been only one decent rush cart to be seen, the rest being smaller vehicles, nicknamed Adam and Eves or Groves, and thus 'mere abortions'. The tradition staggered on into the 1880s in Rochdale, the early '90s in Uppermill and Saddleworth, but by the turn of the century there was no shortage of obituarists to welcome its passing. 'The rushcart was a thing of beauty, but the evils it brought in its train were such that it would not be desirous to have the old custom revived,' said the *Manchester Evening News* in late August 1905. 'The Lancashire operative has discovered a better way of utilising the few fleeting days of his annual holiday.' The *Rochdale Observer* of the same week was equally dismissive: 'The passing of the rushbearing custom is not to be deplored. The Rochdale workers who have gone to the seaside this week to breathe the wholesome sea air are probably spending their time and money far more profitably than did their forefathers when rushbearing came round.'

The new spirit of the holidays, respectable family fun rather than a boozy bonanza, was captured in a poem called *Rachda Wakes*, written by 'Th' Owd Weaver', John Trafford Clegg, in about 1890:

> Come, Betty, lass, it's Rachda Wakes;
> Let's ramble into th' teawn,
> An' feed o' brandy snaps an' cakes,
> Wi' pop to wesh 'em deawn.
>
> There's bobby-horses, dhry lond sails,
> Pikin' folk up i' crops,
> Quack docthors wi' o' maks o' tales
> An' likeness-takkin' shops.
>
> There's shootin'-galleries so long
> 'At nobry th'end con see;
> Blowing machines for wynt-pipes sthrong,
> An' swing-boats flyin' hee.
>
> There's cowd ice-crem, thin lemonade,
> Black puddin's boilt an' fried,
> Wot peighs, ham sangwidges, cake brade,
> An' lots o' things beside.
>
> But that's o' nowt to th' penny shows —
> We'll goo to them o' reaund;
> An' there's a circus, too, tha knows,
> On th' cattle-market greaund.
>
> Th' fat woman's comm again, an' th' pig,
> Th' wild-beast show, wi' th' owd smell;
> An' Buckskin Billy playin' tig
> Wi' Indians o' on th' yell.
>
> Aw'll buy thee sich a fairin', lass,
> As tha's ne'er had afore;

An' tha'll be th' prattiest theere, bi th' mass,
Though there'll be mony a score.
An when it's o'er Aw'll link thee wom,
Through quiet fielt an' lone,
An' afore another wakes con come
Wi' cwortin' we'll ha' done.


It is interesting that Clegg should have singled out 'likeness-takkin' shops' as one of the delights of Rochdale Wakes, since many of our forefathers must have had their first photographs taken in family groups at the wakes or one of the other big annual fairs. Not far from Rochdale and 'Th' Owd Weaver's' home village of Milnrow, even such a modest tourist attraction as Hollingworth Lake boasted several photographers' booths when the poet was a child in the 1860s, and business seems to have been brisk. A potent selling line, and one the cameramen were not slow to exploit, was the comparative cheapness of life in those times, especially among little children. A souvenir, a keepsake, a memento. . . . There is something almost wistfully Victorian about all those words for something by which to remember a loved one – and one has only to look into the eyes of the subjects of those early pictures to know that this was an exercise for posterity rather than a spontaneous holiday whim.

Though changing times and attitudes finally began to win the day against riotous assemblies in and after the 1860s, many  forces of authority made real efforts to stamp on the old customs from the late eighteenth century onwards. Down in the Potteries, Josiah Wedgwood grumbled that 'the wakes must be observed though the world was to end with them', but he had no more power than lesser-known employers to stem the rush for the door at holiday times. Before long an uneasy truce emerged, a compromise based on the often very sensible principle that if you can't beat 'em, join 'em. By the mid-nineteenth century one way the masters could be seen to be joining the men was by organizing works excursions on the new-fangled and exciting railways at holiday times, stressing team spirit and interdependence by means not far removed from tactics with which American- and Japanese-owned companies seek to raise morale and productivity in Britain today. A way in which the men could be seen to be joining the masters was by condoning the sacking or fining of small numbers of key workers whose absence from work had brought annoyance and financial loss to large numbers of their colleagues. So it was that from the 1840s, the relative sophistication of the third and fourth generations of mill owners and workers paved the way for more formal holiday arrangements to be thrashed out, with a greater emphasis on breaks in July and August.

These trends in Lancashire have been chronicled in detail by Dr John Walton of Lancaster University, a leading authority on wakes week history and lore. He points out that Bolton's annual Whitsun holidays were augmented by an August break as a direct result of seaside trips organized by the operative cotton spinners' association, and in Burnley he has traced the inexorable rise of the July fair weekend to four days by the mid-nineteenth century, five by 1870 and a full week for textile workers by 1899, along with an additional long weekend in September introduced in 1890. Oldham and Darwen enjoyed full weeks as early as 1889, Chorley, Nelson, Burnley and Blackburn followed in the years up to 1901, and by 1905 only Bolton with its abiding Whitsun tradition and a few smaller towns had less than a week's holiday in July or August.

Dr Walton wrote the following in the *Economic History Review* of 1981:

Lancashire cotton workers had longer consecutive recognized summer holidays at an earlier date than anywhere else in industrial England and their observance of a regular working week for the rest of the time made it easier for them to save and prepare for a seaside holiday, rather than losing working time and spending surplus cash on more immediate gratifications close to home. . . . By the 1890s whole towns had a deserted appearance at the wakes, with shops closed and churches having to join forces to raise even the semblance of a choir for Sunday service. The fairgrounds persisted, but they were frequented more by people from the surrounding villages than by the townsfolk themselves.

Dr Walton's research shows that as in Lancashire, the Yorkshire woollen towns were switching away from Whitsun to high summer holidays in the 1870s and '80s, and that by then four-day breaks by the sea were common:

But only a single extra day had been added in most places by the turn of the century, and the wakes week was still a thing of the future. The West Riding textile district lagged ten years behind the cotton towns in this respect. Train services seem to have been no more expensive or inconvenient than from Lancashire, and the reasons for the disparity are probably to be found in lower family incomes and the lack of a deep-rooted tradition of seaside visits.

In Lancashire, on the other hand, working people had been treating themselves to the elsewhere almost totally upper- and middle-class delights of a day's bathing by the sea from before the dawning of the railway age – a phenomenon that can perhaps be compared with the hiking and cycling cult of the 1920s and '30s, which was nowhere stronger than in Manchester and its surrounding towns. Not that sea bathing by any social group had any lengthy pedigree. If you discount King Canute and his famous dip, George III at Weymouth was the first monarch to chance the waves, performing the feat in style to the accompaniment of a chamber orchestra. George IV risked the pebbles of his beloved Brighton to take to the water there, but it was not until 30 July 1847 that a ruler took to the sea simply for the fun of it, rather than for supposed medical benefits. 'Drove down to the beach with my maid and went into the bathing machine, where I undressed and bathed in the sea (for the first time in my life), a very nice bathing woman attending me,' Queen Victoria wrote in her diary that night. 'I thought it delightful until I put my head under the water, when I thought I should be stifled.'

The first seaside resorts sold themselves to the rich as substitute spas as early as the late seventeenth century; Scarborough, being able to boast a genuine mineral spring, was very much in the vanguard. At the height of the spa fad in the middle 1700s along came one Dr Richard Russell, whose learned research had suddenly revealed to the world that whether drunk or bathed in, sea water could cure every ill from gout to gonorrhoea, and that was an excuse to build assembly rooms and kursaals and all the other paraphernalia of genteel resort-hood. It also spawned that peculiar phrase 'watering place', with which seaside towns with pretensions graced themselves until well into this century. Indeed, ten minutes among the brochures at the tourist information centre would probably reveal that one or two still do. It is also a pleasant phrase, conjuring up images far more happy than the reality of naked or scantily clad toffs, stricken with boils or jaundice or whatever, being manhandled into the water by insolent helpers. This was a spectacle distasteful to more discerning onlookers from the start - but not nearly so distasteful as what befell their eyes from the 1840s onwards, when the railways struck out to the big coastal towns and the hordes began to descend as night follows day. It is hard to describe the tidal wave that engulfed towns like 'the Queen of the Watering Places'

Scarborough, Southport, Blackpool and Bridlington as the trippers poured in, or to do justice in words to the changes they brought. Doubtless a small number of people reading this book will remember the Spanish fishing port of Benidorm in the 1950s or the beaches of the Portuguese Algarve in the early '60s, and they will begin to have some first-hand insight into the transformation of the English coast in the last century. Many more will know the feeling of outrage at seeing woods and fields where they played as children buried under concrete, brick and tarmac, but this takes no account of the shock felt by the middle classes at the sight of millions of people assumed permanently imprisoned by poverty suddenly on the move for the sheer time and money wasting fun and hell of it. The hymn book reflected widespread thinking with:

> The rich man in his castle,
> The poor man at his gate,
> God made them, high or lowly,
> And ordered their estate.

As a result, it was hardly surprising that the sight of the clogs and shawl brigade besieging the rich man in his sand castle was one that shook establishment Britain to the roots. It certainly brought about a change of policy on the *Southport Visiter*, a newspaper set up almost exclusively to inform its readers who was in town that week. Tens of thousands of Mr and Mrs Ramsbottoms with their children had played little part in this original grand design, as the paper was quick to recognize; the upshot was that it changed tack and has survived to this day, along with the quirky spelling of its name.

As for the question of how so many people could afford these holidays without pay, the answer was 'surprisingly easily' in many cases. With women so widely employed in the mills, the Northern textile trade could be said almost to have pioneered the concept of the double-income family, and at a practical level 'going-off' clubs helped families to spread their saving for the big week over the year. Paid holidays were almost unheard-of before the turn of the century in what is now known as the private sector, especially for manual workers, and no great steps were made in that direction until 1911, when the TUC took them up as a cause; until then the unions had been too concerned with better wages and conditions to devote too much energy to this particular side-issue, and indeed, some had seen them as counter-productive and an excuse for the employers to keep wages down. The pioneers, often with restricted schemes with strings attached, tended to be in the chemical industry or well-known enlightened employers like the soap makers Lever Brothers of Port Sunlight, and Mather and Platt, the giant engineering company based in Manchester.

But while these were benefits enjoyed by the few before the First World War, there were still times when a working man with regular hours could feel quite flush in life – usually at the age of about 45, when he might have had six or seven children aged from 13 to 25 all earning, and contributing their bit to the family coffers. In 1885 the average earnings of an adult male in manual work were about £60 a year. But seven years later, the German sociologist von Schulze-Gaevernitz found that in six out of seven working-class budgets he studied there was enough to spare for some kind of holiday. A weaver in Darwen and his wife, on £100 between them and with three other mouths to feed, could afford no such luxury; but a Bacup weaver with all seven children earning found he could save £50 of his £168 income a year, some of which he was happy to spend on holidays, and an Oldham mule spinner allocated £15 of his £206 income to 'other expenses' in general and a wakes holiday in particular. Best off of all was a fustian cutter from Hebden Bridge with six children all earning, who was able to save £70 a year out of £244 and enjoyed up to 20 days' holiday a year. Figures like these are a reminder that if you worked assiduously at the mill – and indeed, at having children – you could hold your head above water well enough, especially with a pinch of that hard-headed thrift for which Lancashire and Yorkshire folk are well known.

Those wakes savings clubs, often rooted in the factories themselves, mutual aid societies or schools, are also a clue; they tell us that going away was no bacchanalian whim but part and parcel of what a steady, regular working man did to show he cared for his wife and children in late Victorian and Edwardian times. In 1913 a survey of fourteen big towns in Lancashire showed that almost £1 million had been saved by their labour force, a significant proportion of which went on the family holiday  – and while unsympathetic critics bemoaned the fact that saving hard simply to blow the cash in a week seemed a perverted kind of thrift, the mill lads and lasses' holidays could scarcely be seen as riotous living. The concept of being 'a good manager' was at the heart of decent family life, as Harry Bradshaw of south-east Lancashire points out: 'They could make a little go such a long way, those men and their wives. Of course, with the wife at home all day, she had ample time to cook cheap meat for hours on end to make it tender, or perhaps she'd take washing in or go out and clean for a couple of hours in domestic service. And they used to say that if you rubbed against money, some of it would rub against you; women who went out cleaning would often come back not just with their pay but with bits and pieces of clothes, not only for the children but for themselves or their husbands. It all went to help.'

When Ada Fearnley of Halifax went away to Cleethorpes with her parents, four sisters and brother in 1921, her father Percy Pollard was a bricklayer earning perhaps a couple of pounds a week. 'My eldest sister Annie was about 13, so she might have been half-time by then at Ladyship Mills, but otherwise my father's was the only income,' she says. 'But on holiday and at home we'd always have good food, lots of fresh vegetables, which you really could get for next to nothing, and good joints of meat, too. My father would tell us six children that what-ever we saved before the holiday, he'd double and we'd share it out day by day while we were away – and he was always as good as his word. Yes, they were good managers all right, both my parents.'

The story is typical. Tim Phillips of Bamber Bridge remembers a song being sung at a Cleveleys concert party in the mid 1950s, a parody of a currently popular tune called *Pittsburgh, Pennsylvania*:

> There's a pawnshop
> On the corner,
> In Yorksheer
> And in Lancasheer . . .

'They were trying to make us sing along, but nobody was joining in with any great gusto,' he says. 'The plain truth was, we were just not a pawnshop society in Yorkshire and Lancashire, we were much more into the tradition of working for what we'd got and neither a borrower or a lender being. Of course there had been no shortage of pawnshops in the mill towns during the Depression, but only people in the most desperate straits had used them. I suppose the concert party people were trying to strike a chord with us, celebrating our triumph over the bad times. Well, our families had overcome the bad times, all right, or at least were still doing their best to do so, but it was damned hard work and saving that was getting us there, not pawnshops.'

When the Cockney sparrers descended on Brighton or 'Sarfend' at the turn of the century there was as often as not a bout of beery fisticuffs before the day was out. Without making outrageous claims about our forefathers' saintly behaviour, sociologists note time and time again that the early Northern trippers, for all the Southport and Scarborough toffs' sense of fear and loathing on their arrival, generally conducted themselves with decency, sobriety and great good humour. Well, truth to tell, I've heard some dodgy tales about my great-great-uncle Eddie, and perhaps you know a story or two about your great-great-uncle Bert; but it seems that those two were very much the exception to the rule. . . .

# CHAPTER 10

# *Englishmen Are Not Frenchmen*

'Less than a century ago Douglas was a little fishing village, and it never forgets that it owes its development into a borough through the advent of holidaymakers. The corporation today is a wealthy one . . .' So read the Isle of Man official guide book of 1948, and for Douglas one could substitute any number of other Northern resorts – Morecambe, Southport, Skegness and of course Blackpool, which spent £1 million-plus each on its seafront, renovations to the Winter Gardens and a park in the inter-war years, as well as hundreds of thousands more on swimming pools and other projects. It is a reminder that while the coming of the wakes holidays transformed individual working towns for one week of the year, the seaside places that welcomed visitors from those towns week after week during high summer were changed forever and continued changing, even in the hard times that brought communities with more conventional means of earning their living to all but a standstill. The fact is that while the impact of Victorian prosperity is well documented and acknowledged in the big Northern industrial centres, with all due deference paid to the towering town halls of Leeds and Manchester, Bradford and Bolton, the achievements of nineteenth-century builders of pleasure palaces out on the coast all too often go unsung. It is not this book's purpose to chronicle every twist and turn of the deals and setbacks and skulduggeries that went into shaping the resorts as we know them today; most of them were all a long time ago, and living memory of simple holiday pleasures is what is under discussion, here. But it was wakes visitors' money, as much as anyone else's, that allowed and encouraged Southport to build the longest pier in the kingdom,

Not too poor for a trip to the sea: a touching picture taken with a folding pocket Kodak in around 1910.

Morecambe to open a pavilion seating 5,000 and Blackpool, as usual, to go over the top in almost every way imaginable. With this in mind, a brief history of these milestones does not seem inappropriate.

Even before the railways, as we have commented earlier, Lancashire working people had built up a remarkable tradition for going to the sea, enduring all kinds of hardship to spend perhaps a day and a night breathing in the fresh salt air. Workers and their families walked from Manchester to Blackpool, or more often rattled along in carts, and once there they put up with appalling lodgings, the kind that make the comic postcard landlady look like Dame Bountiful. 'A single house here and not a large one frequently receives 120 people to sleep in a night,' wrote one observer in 1813. 'Five or six beds are crammed into each room, and five or six people into each bed; but with every art of packing and pinioning, they cannot all be stowed at one time; those, therefore, who have the places first are roused when they have slept through half the night to make way for another load – and thus everyone gets his night's rest.' The trend continued into Victoria's reign until in 1838, still the best part of a decade before the railways struck through to the coast in the

Blackpool in 1840, five years before the railway.

Formal splendour at the North Euston Hotel and Baths at Fleetwood, 1857.

North, William Howitt was able to record: 'The better class of operatives in the manufacturing districts consider it as necessary "to go to the salt water" in the summer as to be clothed and fed for the rest of the year. From Preston, Blackburn, Bolton, Oldham and all those spinning and weaving towns you see them turning out by the whole wagon and cart loads bound for Blackpool and such places.'

Accounts like these cast fresh light on the conventional wisdom that it was the railways that opened the floodgates to the seaside. It was, of course, but it is clear that in Lancashire before their arrival those gates were already being pounded, if only by determined long-distance walkers in clogs. In the event, the Southern resort of Brighton, at that time a place of fading importance in the wake of William IV's attachment to it, was the first major seaside town to join the spreading rail network, linking with London in 1841. But the North was not far behind, and by the mid-1840s Blackpool, Southport and Scarborough were all on the bandwagon. A broadsheet put around the last town, by then a well-established and genteel spa, cast doubts on the trains' ability to pay for them-

Genteel watering place: Southport in 1865.

selves and insisted that 'the watering place has no wish for a greater influx of vagrants and those who have no money to spend'. It was a familiar cry around the coastline in the middle years of the last century, and again it brings to mind poor King Canute, who was swamped trying to stem the tide; by the time Skegness and Mablethorpe were plugging themselves into the system in the mid-1870s the battle had been well and truly won and lost. The Bank Holiday Act of 1871 was hugely influential in encouraging trippers to take excursions to the sea in August, and in the North, as we have seen, hard-won local agreements gave working people increasing opportunities to get away as the last century drew to an end. Holidays with pay were another matter, with only three million wage-earners qualifying for a week's entitlement before the Act of 1938 boosted that figure to 11 million for the 1939 summer season; not the best of timing, in view of the summers to come in the early 1940s, but at least the last sunny weeks before the war saw millions enjoying a few decent days away for the first time in their lives.

Though Scarborough was not proof against the vagrants, it has not shaken off that touch of gentility – and neither have Southport or

The year the railway came: Morecambe in 1850.

Spinning into history: Blackpool's Gigantic Wheel awaits demolition in this photograph of the late 1920s.

Another packed trip for the *Yorkshireman* at Bridlington in the golden years.

Morecambe, for that matter. Blackpool, Douglas and Bridlington were never afraid to be bright, breezy and boisterous, but from the start there were major resorts that tended to attract older people or families with small children, as well as a host of smaller ones that developed alongside larger neighbours. For Blackpool it was Cleveleys – Lytham and St Anne's, genteelly residential, being a different kettle of fish again, and communities with no place in a book of working people's wakes week memories. Scarborough had the sands and classic fishing harbour of Whitby on its doorstep; those who deemed Llandudno too crowded could turn to Colwyn Bay; and if any gentle soul found the exotic delights of Morecambe too hot, he could always cool down a little at Heysham. The way these resorts developed over the years was not coincidental. For the likes of Blackpool there was simply nothing to lose – and a mighty new industry to be gained on wastelands of sand dunes on either side of the village. If 10,000 visitors a day would bring in £2,000, then twice that number would bring in twice as much – and that would be twice as good. That, in a nutshell, was the Blackpool philosophy from Day One, and it is one from which it has rarely wavered. That is why, to this day, people who go to Blackpool knowing they will hate it come away saying: 'Yes, I did hate it – but don't they do what they set out to do well?' There is a parallel in the 1990s with the American

Disney theme parks – utter and uncompromising self-belief and commitment bringing their rich rewards, with no time wasted on pondering the objections of the intellectual or the snobbish.

In Scarborough and Southport the wishes of landowners and an established middle-class community in resisting shanty towns of amusement stalls and cheap boarding houses were allowed to enter into the formula early on – and the result is obvious. As traditional seaside resorts they have a more broad appeal than Blackpool with their well-to-do and airily planned shopping streets to complement their pleasure grounds and sands – yet in the visitor number stakes, the only figures that the Blackpool impresarios understood or wished to understand, they are measurably less successful than their big, brassy rival with its Tower, giant funfair, three piers and seven miles of golden sands.

Blackpool set so many records. It introduced electric lighting to the Promenade as early as 1879, just to please and amuse the visitors, and anyone who has sat on the front in a fairy-lit five-mile queue in mid-October, condensation streaming down the car windows, knows what that bright idea led to. Its electric street trams, launched in 1885, blazed the trail in England, and it boasted three piers by 1893. The first, the North Pier, was a veteran of 1863, while the second, now the Central Pier but at that time the South Jetty, followed five years later in 1868;

The band pulls the crowds into the Floral Hall Gardens at Southport in the late 1930s.

this was where a long landing stage, now demolished, once thronged with trippers off regular steamboats from Liverpool, Barrow via Fleetwood, Llandudno, Lytham and Morecambe. The name was changed to the Central Pier when the Victoria was opened south of it early in 1893. In 1871 a consortium of businessmen from Blackpool and Halifax set up the Raikes Hall Park, Gardens and Aquarium, a formal 51 acres of 'improving' conservatories and concert halls, as well as provision for dancing, firework displays and pageants. The original concept was not far removed from the spirit of the Great Exhibition of 1851 – but within three years and with a liquor licence covering the whole park, the general talk in the town was of the prostitutes and pickpockets who earned a living there, rather than of the glories of the Empire. All investment after that went into pleasure rides like mechanical racehorses and a miniature railway, families rolled in and business looked up dramatically.

The 1890s was the key decade, with the building of the 518 ft Tower and its various other attractions down on terra firma – the circus that decades later made a legend of the clown Charlie Cairoli, the ballroom that sent the organist Reginald Dixon's name Wurlitzing round the world; then there was the opening of the 220 ft Gigantic Wheel in 1896 and the cultural transformation of a Winter Gardens that had been touted as a genteel and educational venture, with promises of a reading room, art gallery and library, when it had been opened in 1878. By the following year those ideals had been modified by the inclusion on the Whit and August holiday weekends of a girl being shot from a cannon, and all pretence at social niceties was abandoned in 1887 when William Holland, an old showbiz pro from the London music halls, was appointed manager. His aim was what Blackpool's aim had always been – to give the people what they wanted – and the Winter Gardens were never the same again. He died in 1895, too soon to see the opening of the Empress ballroom, into the planning of which he had poured so much time and energy. But by that time Blackpool was established as a brand leader in mass entertainment, and only the World Wars checked the resort's rise and rise from then on. In the mid-1930s it was leaving its rivals standing by attracting seven million visitors yearly between June and September; another milestone was reached in the July of 1945, at the height of the euphoria at the end of the Second World War, when 102,889 trippers rolled in by train in a single day.

The pier at Southport, all 1,200 yards of it, was opened in 1860, with a landing stage for steamers to Llandudno, Douglas, Barrow and elsewhere. It was too long for most people to walk cheerfully – but on the other hand it was too short for the resort's ever-retreating sea, and by

1868 it had been extended another 260 yards, holding the record as Britain's longest pier for nearly thirty years until Southend outstripped it in 1897. The pleasure boats gave up the unequal struggle in 1923 and fires, the bane of so many seaside pleasure projects, took their toll in later years, the last in 1959. Today the pier, at 1,211 yards, is all but back to its original length, a listed building within twenty years of its 150th anniversary – and in scant danger of being swept away by raging seas.

Morecambe, then known as Poulton-le-Sands, was a popular steamship resort from the building of the old pier in the 1830s; but anyone familiar with Morecambe knows that reliable tides are not its strong point, and by the time the railway came through to the would-be waterfront in the comparatively late year of 1850, its days as a port for Scotland, Ireland and even as far as the Baltic and Spain were all but over. From the start, the trippers who poured in were as much from Yorkshire as from the South Lancashire mill towns, who never saw the point of paying more to go to Morecambe when the already well established resorts of Blackpool and Southport were closer to hand. 'Bradford-by-Sea' and 'Little Bradford' the place was known as before the end of the last century, though folks from Leeds and Halifax, too, loved the scenic route via Skipton, Hellifield, Settle, Bentham and Carnforth. That was Morecambe's great bonus, the hills and scenery around, and it did not flinch from being compared with the Bay of Naples or described as the Golden Gateway to the Lakes. At the same time it knew it had to compete with its rivals down the coast, and before the end of the century it was equipped with the baths, aquarium and Winter Gardens type of complex without which no resort was seen as complete. There was a flimsy tower in the early years, too, and a more ambitious one in the first years of this century, a circular pyramid looking more like an overgrown helter-skelter. Its prospectus of 1898 described 'A tower 232 feet high, upon a scale somewhat in excess as regards attractiveness and different in construction to the towers of Blackpool and Paris.' This was rather a cheeky and outrageous way of saying 'lots smaller and more boring', and it is doubtful whether Morecambe Tower would ever have been any kind of success. In the event we shall never know, for a combination of an Act of God in the shape of a lightning strike and the folly of man in the shape of the First World War, which robbed it of its upper steelwork for armaments, ensured that its pulling power was never put to the test. The Central Pier has proved more durable. Built in 1869 and falling victim to yet another fire in 1933, it was rebuilt and remains a focal point of entertainment at a resort that today boasts such attractions as a super leisure dome, Wild West theme park and a major steam railway centre. Then

Watering place delights at Scarborough: the Spa Saloon and Grounds, and St Nicholas Cliff and Spa Bridge.

there are the illuminations at Happy Mount Park. The contrast with Blackpool's mile after garish mile could scarcely be greater, but their pulling-power from August through to the Hallowe'en Spectacular at the end of October is as potent as ever.

Scarborough's answer to the Winter Gardens craze was the Spa Saloon, opened in the 1880s to house the iron-rich mineral springs that had first launched it on its way to prosperity more than a century earlier. These were surrounded by just one of a number of pleasure grounds beside its handsome bay, and throughout its history the resort has clung to its reputation for catering for a more discerning, outdoors-loving clientele. In 1913, with storm clouds looming all over Europe, 'the Queen of the Watering Places' was selling the peace factor heavily – Rich In Natural Beauties, The Finest Marine Drive In Europe, Beautiful Gardens By The Sea. It was also said to be The Children's Paradise, but one was presumably expected to read between the lines and conclude that these would not be the kind of children who would kick sand in your face as they dashed around the beach, or drop dollops of ice cream on your nose. It seems the only blip in this long history of gentility came in the 1850s and '60s, when the loftily devil-may-care resort of old was learning to come to terms with its new status as a magnet for tens of thousands from the West Riding mill towns, poor but honest and becoming imbued by the spirit of late Victorian morality. A letter to the *Scarborough Gazette* in 1866 complained that 'hundreds of men and women may be seen in the water – the men stark naked and the women so loosely and insufficiently clad that for all purposes of decency they might as well have been naked too.' Another writer to the *Gazette* fulminated against the so-called French style of mixed bathing in new-fangled costume, rather than as nature intended, a taste  apparently pioneered in Britain – not in raffish Brighton or Southend but Llandudno: 'Englishmen, be it remembered, are not Frenchmen, and when they go to bathe they go in order that they may enjoy, as unencumbered as possible, a manly and health-giving exercise. As for dancing the quadrilles and such pastimes, which the French indulge in in the water, surely these may be deferred to other and more fitting opportunities.'

There was never much dancing the quadrilles in New Brighton, the rough and boozy Victorian trippers' paradise across the water from Liverpool, though it was proud of its ballroom, which could take 1,000 couples, as well as a splendid 3,000-seat theatre. Most of all it was proud of its Tower, opened in 1900 – and no wonder, for this is one of the great lost buildings of England, on a scale to be spoken of in the same breath as that other fleeting monument to Victorian engineering, the Crystal

Fresh air attractions at Scarborough: North Bay and Peasholme Lake.

Crowds venture out after the rain in Blackpool, *c.* 1910.

Palace. At 621 ft, it was 103 ft higher than Blackpool, and its devotees swore the view from the top was vastly more interesting – the sweep of a Liverpool Bay abuzz with shipping bound for every corner of the world, and on a clear day, the mountains of North Wales, so close you felt you could reach out and touch the peak of Snowdon. It was neglect during the First World War that led to the Tower being laid low in 1921 – but more cruel than that to the town and its environment were pollution in Liverpool Bay and changes in current brought about by the opening of Seaforth Docks that despoiled a beach of clean, firm sand. New Brighton still has its friends, of course, and its attractions – but in spite of being a near neighbour of millions of working people, it missed out on the big times in the golden years of the wakes, and was in no position to put up any kind of fight as a major resort after the Second World War; by the time its pier was demolished in 1973 it was a matter of concern only for conservationists, rather than showmen, and today residents have one of the most handsome promenades in the North mainly to themselves for large parts of the year. Most of them seem happy enough that way.

# CHAPTER 11

# *Pal Of My Cradle Days*

Blackpool, the 1990s – and what survives of the wakes mecca of the golden years? The answer is quite a lot, if you are looking for it – and indeed, even if you are not, because seaside resorts thrive not only by being progressive, which they all claim to be, but by being conservative, too. It is all very well boasting new attractions season by season, but if you shed what brought people to you in the first place there will come a time when you will lose their loyalty. In Blackpool this has not happened, and there is no sign that it will. It is still as fully dedicated to its aim of being the best seaside resort in the country – forget the country, the world – as it was a century ago. And it does it all with such a simple formula that it will take a social revolution far greater than anything we have experienced in the past thirty years to throw it off course.

In the early summer of 1992 Blackpool still has its seven miles of golden sand, not to mention its Golden Mile of catchpennies. It still has the Tower and the Winter Gardens, though between the two these days there are smart new brick-built shopping malls to remind the visitor that even the would-be leisure capital of Europe can be bland and boring in parts, too. Then again, was it not always the case? Who ever heard anyone come home from Blackpool and rave about the lovely shops, as they did after visits to Southport or Scarborough or Llandudno?

Shopping, like *haute cuisine*, is not what Blackpool is all about, though there are a few exceptions to prove that rule. And apart from the sands and the Tower, the Winter Gardens and the seafront sideshows, what else would the timewarp visitor from 1935 recognize? The piers, the Pleasure Beach, the Zoo, Yates's Wine Lodge, most of the big hotels, the art deco Manchester pub, the trams, the lights, the landaus, the tantalizing mingling of chip fumes and the aroma of horse dung on the

135

Golden Mile, the donkeys; even a fair stab at a replica of the Gigantic
Wheel has sprouted on the Central Pier, but as the Victorian original
was taken down in the late 1920s, that is one modern-day attraction that
would be new to a time-traveller from a mere sixty years ago. The
Sandcastle indoor pool and leisure centre is another innovation, as are
the sweeping away of Central Station and the acres of tarmac parking
that dominate the old railway land at the end of the M55 motorway. By
my reckoning, the above list adds up to a comprehensive victory of the
tried-and-tested over the wildly innovative – and since Blackpool now
welcomes 16 million holiday visitors a year, it is fairly clear that that
policy is not very wide of the mark.

The Golden Mile: tradition certainly reigns there. The freak shows are
gone, but life still goes on swimmingly at the Sea Life aquarium with its
great fishy mural and its wonderful selling line 'Sharks In Blackpool –
Dare You Miss Them?' Looking at the scene of feverish street-level capi-
talism all around, the real question is surely what it has always been
along the Mile: Can You Miss Them? Another long-term survivor is the
Waxworks, its Chamber of Horrors allegedly more horrible than ever –
which it needs to be, since it has fierce competition just a couple of doors
away in the Movie Magic Horror Exhibition under the huge effigy of a
gorilla. As I was hurrying by, a large man in a leather jacket handed me
a leaflet telling of the joys of Movie Magic – The Hellraiser Experience,
Moving Werewolf, Demons, MUCH, MUCH MORE – and I assured him
that I would be back to sample these delights when I had more time.
'You just do that,' he replied in a voice so laden with menace that I
gained the distinct impression that if I failed him, the next time I would
be seen thereabouts would be starving in a barrel under a day-glo poster
proclaiming:

> He Said He Would Return
> He Broke His Solemn Vow
> Destined To Repent Unto Death?

Gypsy fortune tellers thrive as predictably as they have always done –
indeed, judging from the fading photographs pinned around their
booths, they are by and large the same soothsayers we remember from
the golden years, transformed from slim, sharp-featured and rather dan-
gerous looking 1950s sirens who might genuinely have lived in Romany
caravans, to well rounded and expensively groomed matrons whose
natural milieu one would guess to be the South Shore penthouse flat

How tickled Hi ham: Ken Dodd, king of the Blackpool shows from the 1950s through to the '90s.

overlooking the sea. Who could have foreseen that forty years in a little box on the front at Blackpool for a few months a year would have brought such visible and outward signs of prosperity? Well, the ladies themselves, presumably. . . . Almost as spooky a timewarp as their pictures of themselves over four decades are some of the showbiz stars into whose mitts they are seen to be peering in the days when Supermac was Prime Minister. Isn't that Frankie Vaughan, whose face this very day adorns the South Pier marquee? It most certainly is, and the number of times you see his image of thirty-five years ago outside gypsy booths up and down the land suggests that he must have spent a whole summer of his comparative youth consulting dusky soothsayers. And isn't that the Ken Dodd of thirty or more years ago, who in a few months' time will be holding the second house at the Winter Gardens in the palm of his hands, probably until about three in the morning, and no doubt with many of the same gags he was telling at the time he was caught by the camera with our gypsy friend?

Fish and chips – with that statutory tang of horse manure from the landaus – are still the staple diet of the Golden Mile, pizzas and burgers lagging a long way behind. Most people round here still eat on the hoof, out of polystyrene rather than newspaper these days, but among the restaurants is one in the shadow of the Tower owned by the Harry Ramsden chain. It is a pleasing little place in traditional, vaguely '30s style, with proper tablecloths and silver service and waitresses with white caps who would not have looked out of place as Lyons Corner House nippies. Harry Ramsden's being a Yorkshire institution, rather than a native child of cod-eating Lancashire, the basic dish is haddock, chips, bread and butter and tea; in May 1992 that meal would have cost you 5p. short of £5 – a point I include simply as a matter of record, since the fact that that would have been the price of your full week's holiday a decade or four ago is neither here nor there.

There is still music to be had on the Mile, not from the nasal song-pluggers loathed by J.B. Priestley and enjoyed by our interviewees Sally Robertson and Doris Smith, but from stalls stacked high with the latest cassettes and CDs. It is the same line of business, I suppose, selling and promoting the sounds of the moment – but it seems to be one that has returned to the Prom and the piers after a couple of generations' absence, since I have no recollection of discs being promoted heavily at the seaside in their heyday of the 1950s and '60s, and indeed no recollection of holidays being a good time for buying records. Perhaps it is all down simply to the nature of the product; records were vulnerable things to pack, while sheet music could come to little harm in your suitcase. When you buy your cassette today it will either go instantly into the Walkman round your neck or the player in your car parked ten minutes' walk away. Not that all Blackpool music has to be straight from the top of the charts. As I passed the music shop at Dale Street Market my eye was caught by a special display highlighting cassettes by George Formby, Gracie Fields, Josef Locke and Al Read; and in the dark and three-quarters deserted Tower Lounge at 3.30 on a bright and breezy Friday afternoon in May, a small audience consisting mainly of elderly ladies on day trips was being entertained by an organist and drummer giving a straight and altogether decent waltz-tempo performance of the old tear-jerker *Pal Of My Cradle Days.*

The customers seemed to be enjoying it well enough, but notably few tears seemed to be being jerked; ladies who have seen seventy Blackpool summers and mill town winters are not always the soft touches the sentimentalists think they should be. But yes, the Tower Lounge open at 3.30 p.m: that indicates one aspect of life that really has changed since the vintage years, for in central Blackpool today, day-long licensing hours reign. No longer is it the bank clerks and the men from the Pru holidaying at Butlin's who can enjoy such delights, to the envy of the outside world – and on a bright off-peak Thursday afternoon at least, it scarcely seemed as if the fabric of society as we know it was about to crumble as a result of it. True, on the Golden Mile you can invest in charming little caps proclaiming 'Drunk? I'm Bloody PISSED', but this would seem to be little more than the 1990s' translation of the Champion Beer Drinker badge that once apparently shocked a Methodist minister on holiday at Butlin's. If you cannot wear a hat like that when you are on a week's holiday in Blackpool with your mates, then when can you?

Down towards the South Shore, film greats are the theme of a stretch of illuminated stars mounted on lamp posts. Tom Cruise, perhaps? Julia Roberts? Tom Hanks? Madonna? Well, no; more Cagney, Chaplin, Temple, Brando, Bogey, Gable, Groucho Marx and Monroe. And of course Blackpool is right – for the moment, at least. Stars were stars in those golden days, and the studio system ensured that they kept in the public eye for decades; today it's hard to recognize many a leading actor from one role to the next, and their freelance status gives them the opportunity to slip away from the limelight after a couple of years and spend their newly-earned millions to their little hearts' content, maybe to return to the screen and maybe not. So two cheers for the illuminations planners for putting Monroe before Julia Roberts – with the proviso that with the current generation of young family couples being able to remember nothing much before 1970, it is not a trick you can pull forever. But then again, who am I to be giving Blackpool tips on drawing in the crowds?

As for the summer shows of 1992, a time-traveller from thirty-five years ago would need no prompting from the gypsy booths to recognize two of the biggest bill-toppers, Ken Dodd at the Winter Gardens and Frankie Vaughan at the South Pier. Other star draws at the heart of the Blackpool tradition were Russ Abbot, Freddie Starr, Mick Miller and the Kaye Sisters, while there was once again the return of the nearest thing to George Formby in the shape of his uncanny imitator Alan Randall. Frank Randle? Well, nobody could imitate him, but at the South Pier, Sunday shows and late-night Saturdays were in the hands of Roy Chubby Brown, back for his sixth season and pushing the bounds of what a comic can get away with just as Randle did forty years ago. 'If easily offended, please stay away' is the health warning that accompanies all his performances, and that could certainly have been said of old Frank, with knobs on. One obvious point of difference is that half of 'Chubby's' shows were on a Sunday night, and that would never have done in the golden years; there seems little room for palm court orchestras and selections from Gilbert and Sullivan on the Sabbath these days – but against this we must set the great disappearing comic postcard mystery at the time of my May visit.

With the demise of long-stay holidays, postcards for home in general are not in demand as they once were. That can be understood, but what did surprise me was the fact that of those on view in the early weeks of the season, only a small proportion were comic – and then, to my eyes, in a rather tame way.

'What's happened to all the saucy postcards?' I asked a young man in a shop under the Tower.

'Nobody seems to buy 'em, so we said we didn't want any this year,' was his astonishing response.

'Bottom fallen out of dirty postcards, eh?' I replied, feeling, even as the words were dying on my lips, like some grotesque reincarnation of those half-sozzled, red-nosed, check-suited, randy-eyed commercial travellers from the comic cards of forty years ago. The weak, inscrutable smile that flitted across the salesman's youthful face told me all I needed to know about why people are not buying saucy postcards any more.

But while the rise and rise of the day tripper means a dearth of decent, or rather indecent, laughs at the postcard racks, what bargains there are to be had in the little back-street boarding houses down towards the South Shore, where cons are still mod and coffee-making facilities in rooms now come almost as a matter of course. 'BBED £60 Off-Peak, £65 Peak' is a typical sign, which sounds pretty good value – and a very good deal indeed when you realise that they mean per week and that BBED means not Breakfast and Bed but Bed, Breakfast and Evening Dinner, the inclusion of 'Evening' being a subtle admission on the land-lady's part that while she knows that all sensible Northern folk have their dinner at dinner time, after a hard morning's work, she being a catering professional has to go through the rigmarole of applying the term to what is really tea. £65 a week half-board, though; it is a remark-able deal, tens of pounds less than what a businessman with a healthy expense account would expect his employer to pay to accommodate him for a single night on the road, breakfast not included. No extra for the use of cruet these days, either, though it is reassuring to peep in through the windows at the breakfast tables and see the Daddies and HP Sauce still in their rightful place. Like so much else on my visit, it was a re-minder that when a resort is oozing with bounce and self-confidence, it can hark to the past and keep itself at the vanguard of the present, too. Blackpool has got this down to a fine art.

# CHAPTER 12

# *Not Morecambe But Majorca*

So where did they go, those golden years of our wakes holidays? They went the way of all history, all the little footnotes of recent history like crystal sets and hula-hoops and ten-bob notes, and all the milestones of global history, the Roman Empire, the wars between the great European powers, the Iron Curtain. They were there and then something came along to change the order of things, something usually called progress but always and forever beyond our control. In the case of the wakes, it was so much. First and foremost, it was the death of the textile trades in our counties of Lancashire and Yorkshire, and the proliferation of other industries. That made it all the more unlikely that we would be working under the same roof as our neighbours. Then there was the motor car revolution of the late 1950s, when the streets in which we traditionally lived and the avenues and closes and drives and crescents in which we were increasingly coming to live suddenly started sprouting little black sit-up-and-beg Ford Pops and Austin A30s outside our doors at night. That made it all the more possible to work not even in the same town as our neighbours, and it certainly took us out of the queues for the trains and buses when holiday time came around. It also made us start thinking about destinations farther afield, a world of farther fields now brought to us nightly by the flickering 12-inch screen in the corner of the sitting room. Bing Crosby going well on Shell in Scotland – not sure about Bing's singing, but Scotland certainly looked worth a visit. Lovers sharing the latest brand of cigarette overlooking the harbour at Clovelly – terrible fags, but we must get to see that little spot. Besides, with the wonders of telly, who needed the pictures any more, who needed the dance hall, the roller-skate rink, the dubious joys of Turf Moor or the Shay or Gigg Lane on a wet and windswept November Saturday? Who needed to be living in the neighbours' pockets for one week a year, let alone fifty-two?

And that was only the start of it. It was now as cheap to fly for a week to Majorca as to go and stay in Morecambe, just as a generation later it would cost less to holiday in Florida than in Florence. In a catchphrase of the times, you couldn't knock it. And when, after a century of constant confrontation, what remained of the local cotton or woollen employers' federations at last agreed with the schools authorities on mutually convenient holidays away from the traditional fairs or rush-bearing or wakes weeks, without the silly business of the kids coming out of school for a fortnight, being back for ten days, and then off again for five weeks, how could you knock that, either? Going away in June if you wanted to, instead of August, when prices were sky-high – you couldn't knock it, could you? Flexi-time, second holidays, moves to other parts of the country for better pay, a taste for sun and Sangria; you couldn't knock it.

At one time it was a small world if you met the girl from the next weaving shed on the front at Filey. Now the spectrum had widened, and you were just as likely to bump into neighbours in Ibiza or Benidorm. Alan Turner of Burnley recalls a chance meeting in Athens in the late 1960s, one that convinced him that however hard you try, you cannot leave home behind for long: 'When the shut-down came that year I went to Greece with a couple of friends, the first time any of us had been abroad. After a few days in Athens we were on a bus, and as soon as the two women in front of us started talking I thought: Colne. What convinced me even more was when one of them got out an embroidered tablecloth she'd bought, and started telling the other how much she'd paid for it. Her friend let her finish, going on about what a bargain she'd got, and then she replied wisely:

'"Ah, yes. But a pound's 30 bob in drachmas."

'I often ponder on this sphinx-like statement to this day, but what struck me about it was the utter Lancashire-ness of it, the combination of watching your pennies, outdoing your neighbour – and a streak of almost surreal daftness. I tapped her on the shoulder and said: "Where are you from, luv?"

'"Ovver near Colne."

'"Yes," I replied. "I thought so."'

Then again, I knew a girl who told a tale about her standing by the control panel in a lift in an Italian hotel when a tanned and glistening vision of manhood walked in and said:

'Could y'press t'fourth flooar, please luv?'

'Gosh, where are you from?'

'Owdham.'

'Oldham? I'm from near Bury. How long have you been here?'

'Two days.'

'Two days? But you're so brown . . .'

And so on and on and on, marvelling endlessly at his sun tan and wondering what lotion he is using until he steps out, and as the lift doors thud back together it is pointed out to her that there are rather a lot of Indians in Oldham these days. An apocryphal tale, one of those so-called urban myths out of the same stable as the granny stolen from the car roof rack or the slimming tablets that turned to worms when they were left on the cooker? Perhaps, but my friend always swore it was true, a sign of changing times on so many levels; all a long way, in any event, from those first exploratory Saturday evenings of the wakes at Scarborough, turning on to the pier and shrieking at some familiar face: 'We came here to get away from you.'

Not that the dying of the tradition is a tale of soaraway success and the rise and rise of affluence. There are many in our towns today for whom two weeks in Blackpool or Scarborough in mid-August, or any other time for that matter, is a dream far beyond reach; and it was a similar tale in the late 1950s, when the textile trades were plunging into their final decline. For all the happy families tootling down to Devon in their Ford Pops, there were others for whom mum and dad's now permanent fifty-two-week holiday without pay meant not even a trip to Belle Vue in the wakes fortnight. The reasons for staying away from the traditional tourist traps could not have been more different but the end result, the absence, was the same. On the first rushbearing Saturday of 1958 the *Rochdale Observer*, on its children's page, surmised that many young residents would be going abroad for the first time, and urged them to be good ambassadors for their town. A couple of pages later the leader column, while wishing travelling townsfolk well whether their destination was Blackpool or Biarritz, pulled no punches in telling the story as it really was – and continued to be:

> This year's rushbearing holiday, a period which in normal circumstances is approached with a delicious sense of anticipation, will be clouded with anxiety for thousands of Rochdalians. The recession in

the cotton trade, coupled with redundancy in some sections of engineering, is the biggest blow the town has suffered for some years, and the threat of even more widespread short-time working in the mills in the near future is bound to put a damper on the expectations of many workers to whom rushbearing is one of the most eagerly-awaited events of the year. The cloud of depression at present hanging over the town's biggest industry is there for all to see, and the cotton workers who have already suffered loss of earnings through enforced short-time working are painfully conscious of all that the slump means in the way of reduced spending power and, possibly, forgoing some of those modest luxuries which have become part and parcel of that higher standard of living to which they have been accustomed in recent years. Whether the cotton operatives and others who are affected by the recession in trade which has hit Lancashire so badly will regard the annual holiday as a luxury which will have to be sacrificed this year remains to be seen. Some will no doubt come to the conclusion, most regretfully, that they will either have to forgo the holiday altogether or at least content themselves with a week's stay at the seaside or in the country, instead of the fortnight on which the 'missus and the kids' had set their hearts . . .

That was thirty-five years ago, and the trend has been constantly away from the town shut-downs ever since then – so what survives? The answer is: possibly more than you would expect. This book celebrates the golden age of the wakes, and I have no hesitation at all in pinpointing the very last days of that golden age to within a couple of years either side of 1960. But that does not mean that all is gone. In several towns, still, those factories that are interdependent continue to share the same holiday week, more often than not at the traditional time – though we must remember that over the years of this century that 'traditional' time has changed within individual communities, in several instances more than once, with a switch from the original late August bank holiday period to an earlier fortnight and a September break being a typical pattern. Though rationalization with the school holidays has taken giant strides in some towns, in others it all stays as confused and messy as ever, and seems likely to remain so. This is no matter of any great pride. In my school days of thirty years ago I would often marvel at how, after more than a century of trying, the education committee and the cotton bosses could continue to make such a complete hash of synchronizing holidays. But it is a reminder, at least, that the tradition still has the legs in it to make an impact on our increasingly uniform and standardized world, even if in this case many of us would prefer it if it did not. Indeed, with consciousness of our heritage and local customs stronger than it has been for generations, there is every reason to believe that it would  take an earthquake to overturn the wakes that have clung on until now. In Rochdale, where all attempts to match the school holidays with the modern-day late June and early July shut-down seem permanently to have been abandoned, they have even revived the rushbearing ceremony. In truth, it is a somewhat genteel affair, with morris dancers and collections for charity and children spreading rushes in church – in spirit much closer to the Victorian church's folksy revival of the tradition than the horrible boozy shenanigans that fell so conclusively from grace 150 years ago. But it is again a reminder of a new consciousness of tradition that can only be applauded, even if an appeal for companies to come forward and sponsor the event is strictly late twentieth century. Even Blackpool Lights are looking for sponsors these days.

A uniform and standardized world; a world of pre-packed supermarket buying and food regulations and European Community directives. Looking back in this book to accounts of the dangers lurking on fairgrounds a couple of generations ago, or that doughty little paddle steamer cutting a swathe through the pleasure boats on Hollingworth Lake, reminds us of just how much we are protected by legislation, how far we have come from the butchers with their wares hanging outside the shop in the smutty air, the flea-ridden beds of seaside digs, and, to return to a constant theme, the days when the only times you could see the hills around you were the occasional summer Sunday or towards the end of wakes week. Yet while our standards of living have risen almost beyond recognition, and our fads in the appliances and means of entertainment with which we ease our lives have moved along with the pace of advancing technology, it is hard to press the claim that we have changed very much in our demands as people in the 150 years since the railways first struck through from our landlocked towns to the coast. I was reminded of just how little during the early season visit to Blackpool reported upon in the previous chapter, a return visit after some five years' absence. My intention was to seek out the sides of life that had altered significantly from the golden years of the wakes – and in the end it was easy to believe that there were none. As has been reflected upon before, we are a conservative lot, by and large, and maybe never more so than on holiday, perhaps because children are the most conservative of us all, and if we return to childhood haunts we want at least to be able to identify with them. Blackpool, being the champion town in England at giving the people what they want, knows this and panders to us with a sure-handedness that falls little short of genius; by constant vigilance and subtle change, it keeps abreast of the times and swaggers along with the same devil-may-care, insouciant grin it wore when George Formby and Our Gracie were the toast of the town.

Of course those of us who can afford it can take two holidays these days – which still leaves plenty of us settling for one, or none at all. Of course day trips rather than prolonged stays dominate the visitor figures of modern English seaside resorts, but that has only sharpened competition between hotels and landladies, meaning that when we do stay we enjoy higher standards than ever before, and keen rates almost unheard-of in inland towns. This, and the end of our collective honeymoon period with foreign holidays, amid the tears of rising oil prices, air traffic control delays and the failure of major travel companies in recessionary times, suggests that the traditional wakes resorts, geared to success, have a few years left in them yet. At Blackpool they are spending £23 million on refurbishing the Tower complex, aim for 1.7 million visitors a year there when the work is complete, and remind all and sundry that a British family of four can have three holidays by the sea here for the price of one in boring old inland Northern France at EuroDisney. The town that lays claim to being Europe's number one holiday destination does not plan to relinquish its title to Mickey Mouse's megabucks in a hurry. And a walk down the packed Prom of any of our resorts on a warm summer evening, with high-spirited Northern voices laughing with friends or singing the songs of the day, or even threatening to give their tired and irritable and sun-itching and skrikin' Wayne a belt round the ear, will be more than enough to convince you that though it now dresses in trainers and shiny tracksuits rather than clogs and shawl, the spirit of the wakes is as cocky and insistent as ever.

It is like the barker on the Golden Mile who accosted me outside the horror show. You think you have outgrown that kind of thing; that freak shows and warm beer and silly hats and scary fairground rides are fripperies of the past, as apparently more sophisticated tastes hurtle you along through life. But just to be on the safe side you say: 'I'm in a hurry now, but I'll come back.'

'You just do that,' growls the ghost of the wakes, the spirit of your childhood.

And of course, like some big kid, you always do.

# BIBLIOGRAPHY

Anderson, Janice and Swinglehurst, Edmund: *The Victorian And Edwardian Seaside* (Country Life, 1978)

Bowman, Winifred: *England In Ashton-under-Lyne* (Ashton-under-Lyne Corporation, 1960)

Briggs, Asa: *A Social History of England* (Weidenfeld & Nicolson, 1983)

Brown, Ivor: *The Heart Of England* (Batsford, 1935)

Butlin, Billy: *The Billy Butlin Story* (Robson, 1982)

Colbeck, Morris: *Yorkshire Laughter* (Whitethorn, 1978)

Colligan, A.W. and Kelsall, George: *The Weighver's Seaport* (G. Kelsall, 1981)

Cross, Gary (ed): *Worktowners At Blackpool* (Routledge, 1990

Davenport, Kathlyn: *Some Oldham Times* (Neil Richardson, 1985)

Freethy, Ron: *Wakes Seaside Resorts* (Faust, 1986)

Harding, Mike: *The Mike Harding Collection: Folk Songs Of Lancashire m* (Whitethorn, 1980)

Hollingsworth, Brian (ed.): *Songs Of The People* (Manchester University Press, 1977)

Hudson, John: *Branching Out* (White Tree, 1989)

Humphries, Steve: *A Secret World Of Sex* (Sidgwick & Jackson, 1988)

Lofthouse, Jessica: *Portrait Of Lancashire* (Robert Hale, 1967)

Mutton, F.C.: *Penguin Guide Derbyshire* (Penguin, 1939)

Opie, Robert: *Rule Britannia* (Viking, 1985)

Palmer, Steve and Turner, Brian: *Blackpool's Heyday* (Palmer & Turner, 1979)

*Picture Postcards From Blackpool* (Palmer & Turner, 1980)

Palmer, W.T.: *Penguin Guide North Wales* (Penguin, 1949)

Pimlott, J.A.R.: *The Englishman's Holiday: A Social History* (Faber & Faber, 1947)

Pomfret, Joan: *The Old Peel Line* (Joan Pomfret, 1972)

Poole, Robert: *Leisure In Britain, 1780-1939* (ed. Walton & Walvin, Manchester University Press, 1983)

The Rambler: *Rambles In The Peak District* (The Rambler, 1934)

Rees, Nigel: *Sayings Of The Century* (George Allen & Unwin, 1984)

Richards, Frank: *Billy Bunter At Butlin's* (Cassell, 1961)

Rothwell, Catherine: *Bright And Breezy Blackpool* (Printwise, 1991)

Searle, Muriel: *Bathing Machines And Bloomers* (Midas, 1977)

Shaw, Joyce: *Down Memory Lane* (Neil Richardson, 1988)

Smith, Morris: *Steam-up In Lancashire* (Whitethorn, 1976)

Stephenson, Tom: *Forbidden Land* (Manchester University Press, 1989)

Trayner, Bernard: *A Short History Of The YHA* (YHA, 1979)

Walton, J.K.: *The Blackpool Landlady: A Social History* (Manchester University Press, 1978)

Walton, J.K.: 'Demand For Working Class Seaside Holidays In Victorian England', *Economic History Review* (1981)

— *The English Seaside Resort: A Social History (Leicester University Press, 1983)*

Walton, J.K. and Walvin, James: *Leisure In Britain, 1780-1939* (Manchester University Press, 1983)

Walvin, James: *Beside The Seaside* (Allen Lane, 1978)

Special thanks are also due to the proprietors of the *Rochdale Observer* and its editor Brian Beal.

# PICTURE
# ACKNOWLEDGEMENTS

Bristol United Press, pp. 3 (top), 20, 55, 56, 137; S.R. Keig, p. 24; National Museum of Photography, p.122; Mansell Collection, p. 2; Oldham Local Studies Library, p. 98; *West Lancashire Gazette*, frontispiece and pp. 4, 7, 14 (top), 18, 45, 134; Wigan Archives Service, p. 100. Other photographs are from the author's collection or by courtesy of Mrs Ada Fearnley, Mrs Joan McKichan and Mr John Thomas.